REACHING NEW HEIGHTS

GOD'S ANSWERS TO YOUNG TEENS' QUESTIONS

VOLUME 4: OCTOBER–DECEMBER

I0138657

DON MEINBERG

LUCIDBOOKS

Reaching New Heights
God's Answers to Young Teens' Questions
Volume 4: October–December

Copyright © 2018 by Don Meinberg

Published by Lucid Books in Houston, TX
www.LucidBooksPublishing.com

Scripture quotations are taken from the Holy Bible, New Living Translation, copyright ©1996, 2004, 2007, 2013, 2015 by Tyndale House Foundation. Used by permission of Tyndale House Publishers, Inc., Carol Stream, Illinois 60188. All rights reserved.

All verses marked with an asterisk (*) are the author's own paraphrase.

ISBN-10: 1-63296-300-0
ISBN-13: 978-1-63296-300-0
eISBN-10: 1-63296-248-9
eISBN-13: 978-1-63296-248-5

TABLE OF CONTENTS

"I have known Pastor Don Meinberg for over 7 years, since the time he planted Reflections Christian Fellowship in Southern California. During that time, I have seen his energy and enthusiasm, not only for God but also for kids. I have read his *Reaching New Heights* series and believe that they are great books for young people going through the tough pre-teen and teenage years. The daily topics are what middle school and young high school kids may experience for the first time, and his format will definitely help kids learn how to use the Bible to deal with problems. These books are needed, especially in today's world."

—Jeff Ludington,
Lead Pastor at Generations Church;
author of *Frustrated: How the Bible Resolves Life's Tough Questions*

"I have known Pastor Don for over 25 years. He has a true love for Jesus and especially for kids. He has worked many years with middle school and high school kids in building them up in the Lord. His book series *Reaching New Heights* is a must-read for any young person going through the difficult years of puberty and beyond. It is a unique book series that gives kids God-centered advice on some difficult topics that they might be experiencing for the first time. Every middle school and young high school student needs this book series to help them answer the tough questions of life in a Christ-centered way. It will bless kids and parents alike!"

—Mark Bridgeford,
Elder, Summit Ridge Church, Rancho Cucamonga, California

"*Reaching New Heights* would be a valuable resource for any pastor, youth worker, or parent's library. As adolescent young brains are developing, they need time to think through the issues of their lives and experience God speaking directly to them in His word. These amazing books provide such a great resource and would bless the lives and homes of Christians with clarity and substance. Best of all, I can see this series being the catalyst for opening lines of communication and dialogue within families and churches. It is highly recommended."

—**Tommy Peterson**,
Youth Pastor, Bethel Baptist Church

"As a fifteen-year-old girl, I find that these books fit right in with the things that happen in school and church all the time. It helps to read what the Bible tells us to do in all these situations and to see the solutions to these difficult issues of life. *Reaching New Heights* contains a wide range of topics and hits the specific audience where things are very relative. It provides Scripture for different learning types and is well-laid-out for each question and answer."

—**Tori Hitchcock**,
Escondido, California

INTRODUCTION

The purpose of this book is to give kids in middle school to high school between the ages of 10 and 15 a place to find God's answers for problems they face daily. There are numerous books and other publications that focus only on high school or college age kids and the struggles and problems they face regarding drugs and alcohol, dating, sex, jobs, and career choices. But my research found very few books that concentrate solely on questions that young teens or preteens face in their everyday lives. Their issues may be similar to the topics facing high school and college age kids but from a totally different perspective. Younger kids may be facing some of these issues for the very first time and are confused and frustrated. Also, their questions are more likely to be about lying to elders, cheating on tests, new friendships, temptations, and difficult choices. This book gives them an avenue to learn what God says about these issues and how to apply God's answers to their lives in a language they can understand.

The book is formatted with an advice-column look with the main topic at the top of the page and the related issue or question directly below. The issues or questions are mainly presented as stories that young teens might be experiencing. But the beauty of this book is that young teens or preteens can revise the story content to fit a similar problem or issue they are encountering that is related to the main topic. They can do that for any of the main topics in the book.

Following each story or issue is a section called "What God Says." It includes the book, chapter, and verse in the Bible that directly relates to the question and main topic. Sometimes, a paraphrase of the verse is used.

It may or may not include the entire verse, depending on the issue. I paraphrase some verses to make it easier for the reader to understand and apply the appropriate meaning of the verse to the subject or question. The Bible translation used in this book is the New Living Translation, chosen for its accuracy and easy-to-read format.

Below the Bible's solution to the issue is the application of God's answer. Sometimes, it is extremely difficult to interpret what the Bible means and apply it to the problem at hand. This section does that for the reader, breaking down God's words into practical terms that young teens can understand and use to solve their own dilemma. Each answer is unique to the question presented and God's solution to that issue.

Once the young teen has read the issue, learned God's solution, and understood its meaning by applying the verse, they are ready for the next section called "Questions to Ponder." Here, we want our young students to write down their thoughts and notes on what they just read. Each topic includes a couple of questions to guide them along in their thinking. This section is a tool that can be used for open discussion among a group of young teens, or it can be used as a tool for individuals to write down their own thoughts and ideas and how they apply to their own situation.

At the top of each journal page is a motto that directly relates to the main topic. The purpose of the motto is to give the reader one final thought on the main topic and hopefully inspire them to remember this topic and solution for a long time. The young teen may not remember the story or the Bible verse, but chances are good that they will remember the motto because it is only one line directed exclusively at the main topic.

There are very few (if any) books available for young teens and preteens ages 10 to 15 that relate directly to them and their needs from a biblical perspective. It takes those difficult issues—prayers not answered, lack of communication with parents—for young teens to understand and apply God's word. This is a book for their level of maturity written primarily for their age group, focusing totally on questions and problems in their lives with useful God-inspired answers. This book will teach young teens right from wrong with a biblical stance on tough issues that would make even adults cringe. This book could become a source of enlightenment for students and an answered prayer for the adults in their lives.

This book can be used in a variety of ways: as a daily devotional for a year, as an advice textbook, as a diary of solutions to teens' problems, or as a memorable book of stories with God's solutions.

OCTOBER 1

OPPRESSION AT SCHOOL

A: I must be the only guy at my school who prays. Every school day, before I take a bite of my lunch, I say a prayer of thanksgiving. Every time I'm about to take a big test, I say a prayer. Every time there's a football game at my school, I say a prayer. Now all the kids in my class are making fun of me because I pray. They mock me about God, saying things like, "God's telling him all the answers" or "Maybe I should give my crappy lunch to God." They insult me all the time and call me names just because I pray. I enjoy praying to God no matter where I am, but I am getting tired of being picked on because of it. Can't God take this oppression from these other kids away from me?

> **What God Says:** Matthew 5:11–12 *God blesses you when you are mocked and persecuted and lied about because you are my followers. Be happy about it. Be very glad. For your reward in heaven awaits you.**

A: The more oppressed you are at school for God's sake, the bigger the blessings and rewards you will receive in heaven. As hard as it might sound, we need to remain obedient to God and endure persecution with patience, just as Jesus did when He was persecuted and ultimately killed on the cross. Whatever you do, don't give up hope. Pray that God will give you the strength to endure and the courage to stand up for God to those who are persecuting you. Nothing comes easy when the reward at the end is so great, and God promises a big reward for his followers in heaven.

Questions to ponder:
How would you handle being oppressed at school?
Do you pray before eating? Why or why not?

Ask God to strengthen your faith.

JOURNAL:
_____

_____
_____
_____
_____
_____
_____
_____
_____
_____
_____
_____
_____
_____
_____
_____
_____
_____
_____
_____
_____
_____
_____
_____

OCTOBER 2

COMMUNICATION WITH PARENTS

Q: I have a very difficult time communicating with my parents. Every time I try to tell them something that happens to me, good or bad, I know I'm going to get a lecture on what they did with the same thing 25 years ago. You see, my mom is the lecturer in the family, and my dad is the fixer. He thinks I want all my situations fixed, when most of the time I just want them to listen. They think what they are doing is right, but all it's doing is driving me away from ever wanting to talk to them. I love my parents, but I need to figure out a better way to communicate, or we'll never speak to each other.

> **What God Says:** James 1:19 *My dear brothers and sisters, be quick to listen, slow to speak and slow to get angry.**

A: You need to have patience with your parents because, believe it or not, it sounds like they love you a lot and want to help you the best way they can. Read the verse above again. The important thing is to be quick to listen and slow to get angry as they try to teach you from their experiences and wisdom. I know it's difficult sometimes to listen to the same lectures and your mister-I-can-fix-anything dad, but they definitely mean well. Ask God to open your heart to their words and truly listen to what they have to say. You may actually be surprised how useful it could be. And if you want them to listen to you and not talk, respectfully ask them to do that. And that applies to you just as much as it applies to your parents!

Questions to ponder:

How would you rate your communication with your parents on a scale of 1 to 10?

Why?

Don't shun communication with your parents.

JOURNAL:

_____

_____

_____

_____

_____

_____

_____

_____

_____

_____

_____

_____

_____

_____

_____

_____

_____

_____

_____

_____

_____

_____

_____

OCTOBER 3
DEALING WITH OVERLY COMPETITIVE KIDS

Q: Do you know someone who is highly competitive and has to win at everything or they get mad? That is the perfect description of my brother. It doesn't matter what game it is. It could be a one-on-one basketball game or ping-pong or even checkers, but he has to win or he goes crazy. Then when he does win, he brags about how much better he is. I do enjoy competing against him because he is good at most things, and playing against him makes me better. But I can truly do without the over-competitiveness and cocky attitude. What can I do to still play against him but not have to put up with his antics?

What God Says: Luke 18:11 *The proud Pharisee stood by himself and prayed this prayer: "I thank You God that I am not a sinner like everyone else, especially that tax collector over there."*

A: Kids who are overly competitive unfortunately do become cocky when they win. People who are over-competitive have good points and bad points. Their good point is that they know how to establish goals and give 100% effort to reach that goal. The bad point is that they are difficult to play against because of their attitude, and if they lose, they get mad. If they win, they are cocky and judgmental, just like the Pharisee in the verse above. God says to play the game to win but with good sportsmanship. If you win, be humble about it. If you lose, recognize your opponent's victory and move on, for there will be other days to win.

Questions to ponder:

How do you deal with overly competitive kids who must win at any cost? Are you a competitive person? Give examples!

Don't be cocky or judgmental when you win.

JOURNAL:

_____

_____

_____

_____

_____

_____

_____

_____

_____

_____

_____

_____

_____

_____

_____

_____

_____

_____

_____

_____

_____

_____

OCTOBER 4

DISABILITY

Q: I am very angry with God. See, I was born premature, and when I came out, I had no arms or legs. So I can't do anything for myself. I even need help going to the bathroom. Why was I born with this horrendous disability? Why didn't God give me arms and legs like all the other kids? I hate it because other kids stare at me all the time. Or even worse, they point and whisper to others about me. I'm mad because I can't play sports that I love or even play a musical instrument. I can't do anything like normal kids can. I can't even play outside or ride a bike or skateboard like everyone else. I just wish I had never been born!

What God Says: 1 Corinthians 7:17 *You must accept whatever situation the Lord has put you in.**

A: Unfortunately, we cannot choose our looks or our form, so we need to accept whatever good or misfortune that comes our way. I know you're bitter with your unfortunate disability, but you are alive, and that is a blessing from God. You need to change your heart, accept whatever situation you are in, and use it to glorify God. There have been countless paraplegics and people with disabilities who have lived wonderful, fulfilling lives using their disabilities as an asset rather than a liability. And with technology today, it is common for kids and adults to get prosthetic arms and legs that allow them to do everything a normal child can do. So don't lose faith and hope in God, because He loves you no matter what your disability is. Remember, your body is only temporary, but your soul is forever!

Questions to ponder:

If you had a disability, what kind of attitude would you have toward life? Would you be angry at God?

Positively accept the things you cannot change.

JOURNAL:

DEALING WITH EMOTIONAL FRIENDS

Q: My friend cries at everything. When someone is mean to her, she cries. When someone looks at her the wrong way, she cries. If she gets a B on a test, she cries. She cries at sad movies or even happy movies. So, one day she came to school looking like she had ben crying. I wasn't in the best mood, so I didn't ask her what was wrong. I figured it was something dumb, so I ignored her the entire morning. It turns out that her cat that she loved so much and talked about a lot saw something, ran into the street, and got hit by a car. I have a special cat, too, so I knew she was hurting. Now, she's mad at me because I wasn't there when she needed me.

What God Says: Proverbs 21:13 *"Those who shut their ears to the cries of the poor will be ignored in their own time of need."*

A: I think it's wrong and extremely insensitive to shun a friend in time of need. I understand your friend's persistent crying can get old and annoying, but if that's her only fault, that's not so bad. It's like the kid who cries wolf all the time. When something important comes up, nobody is there to help. God teaches us to be sensitive and compassionate to the emotions of others and not shut our ears to their cries. Talk to your friend and apologize for your behavior. Then, calmly explain why you reacted like you did. It's always better to err on the side of sensitivity than on the side of uncaring.

Questions to ponder:

How do you handle emotional friends?

How do you help them?

Have you ever shunned emotional friends by accident?

You need to be there when your friend is hurting.

JOURNAL:

_____

_____

_____

_____

_____

_____

_____

_____

_____

_____

_____

_____

_____

_____

_____

_____

_____

_____

_____

_____

_____

_____

_____

_____

HELPING KIDS MAKE GOOD DECISIONS

Q: My friend got invited to a concert of her favorite band on the other side of town. She was so excited when she found out that another kid got a ticket for her. The problem is that my friend is only 12 years old, and the kid who got the ticket is 16 years old. There is no way her parents will allow her to go to the concert. They will say the boy is too old and the concert is too far away, and since it's a rock band, they will say the crowd will be too crazy. So my friend decided to lie to her parents and say she's at my house spending the night. Then, she will go to the concert and come back to my house while I cover for her. Her other choice is to tell her parents the truth and take her chances that they will let her go. I begged her to do the latter, but she decided to lie to her parents and go to the concert. What should I do now?

> **What God Says:** Proverbs 12:15 *Fools think they need no advice, but the wise listen to others.**

A: If we reject the advice of a wise person, just like your friend did, she is probably making a very foolish decision. We need to listen to sound advice and weigh it carefully, and then we will make better choices. I think your friend made a foolish choice by going to the concert when she knows her parents would disapprove. You are put in a tough position of lying to her parents to cover her bad decision or risking your friendship and telling the truth. If you cover for her, she'll do it again and again and again. If you tell her parents the truth, you'll probably lose a friend. Pray to God about what to do. But God is all about truth, and He will never support lying to help a friend.

Questions to ponder:

Do you give good advice?

Is it hard to tell your friends no?

Give examples in detail.

Taking good advice usually leads to wise decisions.

JOURNAL: _____

_____
_____
_____
_____
_____
_____
_____
_____
_____
_____
_____
_____
_____
_____
_____
_____
_____
_____
_____
_____
_____
_____
_____

FAMILY ISSUES

Q: My family is in a state of chaos right now. Everything that could go wrong with my family is going wrong. First of all, my mom told my dad that she's having an affair with a guy at work. Instead of getting angry and doing something about it, my dad said and did nothing. Then, my brother stole the family car, took it on a joyride for three days, ditching school, only to come back home with a big dent in the back bumper. Again, my dad said very little and did nothing. Finally, my younger sister got expelled from fourth grade for cheating and then bringing a knife to school. My dad got a little angry but did nothing. Our family is going crazy, and my dad doesn't seem to care.

What God Says: 1 Timothy 3:4 *He [a father] must manage his own family well with children who respect and obey him.**

A: God has appointed fathers to be the spiritual leaders of the family. When a father fails at that responsibility, the whole family suffers. In your family, your dad is not taking a leadership role to help in times of trouble. You need to talk to your dad about taking control of these issues and being the man that God wants him to be. In those families with no fathers, the mom must take on that role as well as the many other roles she already has. Your family will continue to be in chaos if your father sits idly by and does nothing. And you will lose all respect for him.

Questions to ponder:

What is the worst thing that has happened to your family?

If nothing comes to mind, what is the worst thing that could happen to your family?

God wants a dad to be the leader in his family.

JOURNAL:_____

_____

_____

_____

_____

_____

_____

_____

_____

_____

_____

_____

_____

_____

_____

_____

_____

_____

_____

_____

_____

_____

_____

OCTOBER 8

DEALING WITH FRIENDS FULL OF EXCUSES

Q: I have been trying to get my friend to go to church with me. But every time I ask her, she has one excuse after another. First, it was her sick grandmother who lived out of town. Another week, it was homework and a big test the next day. Two weeks ago, she said she was tired and just didn't feel like it. Then, just last week was the best excuse. She said she wouldn't go to church because her parents don't go and she doesn't think it's right. I've gotten to the point that I'm tired of hearing all these lame excuses, and I'm just going to give up trying.

> **What God Says:** Romans 1:20 *From the time the world was created, people have seen the earth and the sky and all that God has made. They can clearly see His invisible qualities—His external power and divine nature. So they have no excuse for not knowing God.**

A: God will accept no excuses for not knowing Him and accepting Jesus as our Lord and savior. All we need to do is look around and see all of His glorious creation. We can't help but marvel at His works. Those who make excuses for not following God and going to church have already made the choice of not believing in Him. There will come a day when your friend will die and wish she was full of love for God rather than full of excuses. We have no excuses; we need to make a choice. But don't give up on your friend, just as God has never given up on us. Read the above verse to her and tell her the time for excuses is past, and it's time to trust in the almighty God.

Question to ponder:

How do you deal with friends who are full of excuses all the time? Does it frustrate you?

There are no excuses with God.

JOURNAL:

_____

_____

_____

_____

_____

_____

_____

_____

_____

_____

_____

_____

_____

_____

_____

_____

_____

_____

_____

_____

_____

_____

_____

_____

GRUDGES

Q: I will never forgive my father for what he has done to my mom. My dad works a lot of hours (or this is what I thought). He goes to work at 6:00 a.m. and usually doesn't come home until after 9:00 p.m. He goes out of town about once a month for about a week at a time. It turns out that my father has been living a double life. You see, he's been dating a woman from work for about a year, going to her house every night, having sex, and just being with her. And these trips he's been taking were also all lies. He never went anywhere; he just stayed at her house the entire week. When my mom found out, she was devastated. I hate my father for what he did, and I will always hate him. I will never get over him ruining our family.

What God Says: Matthew 6:14–15 *"If you forgive those who sin against you, your heavenly Father will forgive you. But if you refuse to forgive others, your Father will not forgive your sins."*

A: What your dad has done to ruin your family is wrong and despicable in the eyes of God. His selfishness and deceit are terrible sins, and I can't blame you for the bitterness you feel toward him. However, God teaches us that He will forgive us without limits and that we should forgive others who have wronged us if they are truly sorry. We all sin, and every sin is evil in the eyes of God. If we can't forgive others, then how do we expect God to forgive our wrongdoings?

Grudges give us power over another, but if God (the most powerful force in our universe) does not hold a grudge against us, then, why should we? Healing begins with forgiveness, so get rid of the grudge and begin your life anew.

Questions to ponder:

Do you hold grudges?

What would you have done if your dad did the same thing as the one in this story? Explain.

Grudges can ruin a person's soul.

JOURNAL: _____

_____

_____

_____

_____

_____

_____

_____

_____

_____

_____

_____

_____

_____

_____

_____

_____

_____

_____

_____

_____

_____

OCTOBER 10

DOUBTS ABOUT SELF

Q: I live in a really poor, tough neighborhood. There is graffiti everywhere, and we hear gunshots at least two or three times a week. We can't go outside at night, and the noises are loud. There are gangs on every street, and we hear the fighting and bottles breaking on a nightly basis. I am currently 12 years old, and I live alone here with my mom. There's a ton of ways to do wrong in this neighborhood. I don't think I'm strong enough to be able to stay out of trouble as I get older. I'm not confident in myself to say no when a gang member wants me to steal something or hurt someone. My mom taught me the difference between right and wrong, but I'm a follower by nature, so it would be easy for me to follow the crowd. I totally doubt my sense of judgment.

> **What God Says:** Jeremiah 17:7 *"But blessed are those who trust in the LORD and have made the LORD their hope and confidence."*

A: You don't ever have to face a situation alone as long as you have God in your life. You're right that it is easy to turn bad, especially in a rough neighborhood like yours. You need to trust in God and let Him shoulder the pressures and burdens of your situation. Let Him give you the strength and courage to face each day with the hope and confidence of doing good. There is nothing that God can't handle. You may have doubts about yourself, but there is no doubt about God's love for you. Pray to Him to keep you strong, and then do what is good and right and pleasing to your father in heaven.

Questions to ponder:

On a scale of 1 to 10, how much confidence do you have in yourself regarding school, skills, and making good choices?

What would you do if you were the boy in this story?

God gives us the confidence to handle anything.

JOURNAL:

_____

_____

_____

_____

_____

_____

_____

_____

_____

_____

_____

_____

_____

_____

_____

_____

_____

_____

_____

_____

_____

_____

_____

DEALING WITH KIDS WHO CAN'T LOVE

Q: Everyone at my school knows about this guy who lives on a bench on a street corner right across the street from the school. He seems to be completely harmless and wouldn't hurt a fly. He just got hit with some bad times (losing his home and his family), and now he's living on the streets. All of us are nice to him, giving him food from our lunches or lunch money so he can buy his own food. We are all nice except my best friend. He is constantly saying rude remarks to him about what a pig he is or how bad he smells. Instead of helping him, my friend laughs at him and insults him. I don't know why he acts that way because this homeless man has never said or done anything to him.

> **What God Says:** Matthew 10:42 *"If you give even a cup of cold water to one of the least of my followers, you will surely be rewarded."*

A: Doesn't your best friend know that any kind gesture you do for someone like that homeless man is the same as doing it for God? God created this homeless man, and He loves him just as much as He loves your friend. Saying rude remarks, insulting the homeless man, and doing mean things to him is the same as doing those things to God. Most people struggle to understand this, but it's true. Jesus repeats the above verse in Matthew 25:40 when He says, "I tell you the truth, when you did it to one of the least of these my brothers and sisters, you were doing it to me!" Tell your friend to stop being mean to this guy and show him the love and respect he deserves.

Question to ponder:

How do you try to help kids who struggle with love?

To love God, you must love all His people.

JOURNAL:_____

_____

_____

_____

_____

_____

_____

_____

_____

_____

_____

_____

_____

_____

_____

_____

_____

_____

_____

_____

_____

_____

OCTOBER 12

LYING TO COVER WRONGDOING

Q: A kid at school figured out a way to get into the teachers' lounge and get a copy of the big science test we were having the next day. So after we took the test, he naturally was the only kid in class to get 100%. But he made one mistake. On the fill-in-the-blank and essay questions, he answered them identically (word-for-word) as the teacher had written them on the answer sheet. The chances of that happening are 10,000,000 to 1. The teacher figured that the kid had cheated, but he had to prove it. The kid lied about everything, using other kids as witnesses who also lied for him. So he didn't get expelled. As a matter of fact, since no one said anything, he didn't even get in trouble for his cheating. I wonder how he got all those kids to lie for him.

> **What God Says:** Romans 1:18 *God shows His anger from heaven against all sinful, wicked people who push the truth away from themselves.**

A: Lying to cover wrongdoing at this young age will lead to nothing but worse trouble as this kid gets older. This behavior is no different than what common criminals do after committing a crime. They do a heinous act and then try to cover their tracks so they don't get caught. Using kids as alibis to lie for him was a coward's way of not taking responsibility for his actions. I bet he promised all those kids who covered for him a copy of the answer sheet for the next test. God hates lying because God is all about love. To use others to get away with cheating is just wrong. I wish someone would have the courage to step forward and tell the truth, or this kid will do the same thing over and over again.

Questions to ponder:

Have you ever lied to help a friend not get into trouble? Explain.

If not, is there a situation that you might? Give details.

Using people to cover your sin is a hideous act.

JOURNAL:

_____

_____

_____

_____

_____

_____

_____

_____

_____

_____

_____

_____

_____

_____

_____

_____

_____

_____

_____

_____

_____

_____

OVERWEIGHT AND GLASSES

Q: I have 20-2,000 vision, so I need really thick, powerful glasses just to see. Even with these glasses, I need to sit in the front of the classroom to see the whiteboard. It also doesn't help that I just love food, and I'm about 100 pounds overweight. So I get teased and laughed at on a daily basis. I don't understand why kids tease other kids because they can't see. I can't help it that I was born with bad eyesight; it's not like I want to be half-blind. But every day, just about the same kids call me four-eyes and geek and fat slob. I get tired of the insults, but I don't know what to do to change my situation.

What God Says: Romans 5:3–4 *We can rejoice, too, when we run into problems and trials, for we know that they are good for us—they help us learn to endure. And endurance develops strength of character in us, and character strengthens our confident expectation of salvation.**

A: Unfortunately, it is almost impossible to change mean kids. If kids want to be cruel and mean, they will find a vulnerable person as a target and go after them. You need to do what the above passage says. Have confidence in yourself to endure the teasing and then use that endurance to develop a strong character, which leads to a better outlook on yourself and life. And this confidence starts with God. You may not be able to change mean kids, but you can arm yourself with the best protection, and that's God's power in you. He will give you the strength and courage to endure this difficult time and make you feel good about yourself.

Questions to ponder:

Why do you think kids make fun of kids who are overweight and wear glasses?

Do you stick up for kids who are teased?

Rely on God's power against mean kids.

JOURNAL:
_____

_____

_____

_____

_____

_____

_____

_____

_____

_____

_____

_____

_____

_____

_____

_____

_____

_____

_____

_____

_____

_____

_____

_____

_____

OCTOBER 14

RETALIATION

Q: Last week, my younger brother got beat up as he was walking home from school by a gang of kids from another street. He came home with a busted lip and a swollen face. He was real upset and crying because he said he did nothing but walk down the street. I was real angry, so I talked to some of my friends on the block and told them what happened. They agreed to help me find a kid about the same age as my brother who was involved in the fight and retaliate. We are going to beat him up the same way they beat up my brother. Then, they will know not to mess with me, my family, or anyone on this block.

> **What God Says:** 1 Peter 2:23 *He did not retaliate when He was insulted. When He suffered, He did not threaten to get even. He left His case in the hands of God, who always judges fairly.**

A: Here is the main problem with retaliation. The street gang hurt your little brother by beating him up, so you get your gang together to beat up one of their kids on that street. Then they get mad and do something worse to someone on your street, and you get real angry and do something really bad (like killing or badly injuring) to another kid on their street, and on and on. The problem is that there is no end to retaliation, and a lot of innocent people get hurt in the process. God teaches us not to retaliate and to try to live like Jesus who did not retaliate when He was being beat and spit on before the cross. Let God be the judge and jury, and don't take matters into your own hands.

Questions to ponder:

In your opinion, is retaliation ever okay?

How would you handle it if your loved one got seriously hurt?

What would you do? Explain.

God loves peace, not war.

JOURNAL: _____

_____
_____
_____
_____
_____
_____
_____
_____
_____
_____
_____
_____
_____
_____
_____
_____
_____
_____
_____
_____
_____
_____
_____

OCTOBER 15

PROCRASTINATION

Q: I have a science project due this week, and I haven't even started. We need to build a visual aid, do an experiment, and then write a five-page essay discussing the hypothesis, experiment, and results. I've known about this project for two months, but it took me a long time to figure out what to do it on. Then, I waited until I finally got the materials for the experiment. Now, the entire project is due in three days, and I don't know what to do. There is no way I can finish it on time, and the teacher has already said no extensions. I wish I wouldn't have procrastinated so long.

> **What God Says:** Proverbs 6:10–11 *"A little extra sleep, a little more slumber, a little folding of the hands to rest—then poverty will pounce on you like a bandit."*

A: Sounds like you have a big problem, but you are not alone. Most kids wait until the last minute to do something they should have done long ago. Procrastination is a form of laziness, and it ultimately leads to disaster. You shouldn't wait until the last minute, because if you do, it will show in your shoddy work and written report. God wants you to be responsible, and start on the task early, and do the best you can. Then you will get the reward you deserve. Remember this: Time is a precious gift that God gives us on this earth. It must not be wasted or squandered, because the consequences are huge.

Question to ponder:

Describe the last time you procrastinated about something and it cost you. Do you struggle with procrastination? Explain in detail.

Time has a way of flying by—don't procrastinate.

JOURNAL:_____

_____

_____

_____

_____

_____

_____

_____

_____

_____

_____

_____

_____

_____

_____

_____

_____

_____

_____

_____

_____

_____

TATTLING BROTHERS AND SISTERS

Q: I have a baby sister who loves to tattle on me. Anytime she sees something I've done wrong, she tells my parents. Or if she hears something that sounds wrong, she tattles on me. She sneaks around the house just looking for things to squeal about. And if I start yelling at her for doing this, she cries to mom and tells her I'm being mean to her. I just can't win! When I complain to my mom about it, she tells me that infamous line, "You are the oldest and should know better." So my little sister never gets in trouble. I can't do anything without her telling someone about it. I'm about ready to strangle her.

What God Says: Isaiah 58:13 *Honor the Lord in everything you do, and don't follow your own desires or talk idly.**

A: People usually tattle or squeal for one of two reasons: first, to hide some wrong they are doing by getting someone else in trouble; and second, for attention. Rarely do kids tattle for the good of someone else. It's usually for the tattler's best interest. Both of these reasons for tattling are not pleasing to God. He calls it idle talk, which means talking but saying nothing productive. In the verse above, God says if you tattle to win your own desire, it is wrong. You need to go back to your mom in a mature, calm manner and explain the wrong your sister is doing. There is nothing good that comes out of tattling at this young age. God is not pleased with the tattler, and the one being tattled on is resentful and full of contempt. Pray to the Lord and try to talk to your mom again.

Questions to ponder:

How do you deal with tattling brothers and sisters?

Does this apply to you?

Tattling at a young age is normally fool's talk.

JOURNAL: _____

_____

_____

_____

_____

_____

_____

_____

_____

_____

_____

_____

_____

_____

_____

_____

_____

_____

_____

_____

_____

SIBLING PROBLEMS

Q: I have a large, blended family. My parents are divorced, and my mom moved across the country, so I'm living with my dad and two brothers. Well, my dad married a woman about a year ago who also has three kids (two girls and one boy). So now there are eight of us living in the same house. The biggest problem is that I don't get along at all with my two stepsisters. First of all, they are extremely mean and bossy and spend hours in the bathroom. We have only three bathrooms for eight people, so you need to be quick. They take all my cool clothes to wear without asking, and they are constantly giving me unwanted advice on my problems. I can't stand having them in my house.

What God Says: Titus 3:2 *They must not speak evil of anyone, and they must avoid quarreling. Instead, they should be gentle and show true humility to everyone.**

A: It is extremely difficult to have peace and tranquility in a blended family, especially one as large as yours. You did not choose this living arrangement, and yet you have to live with it. Your stepmom and dad need to take charge of the situation. This arrangement is uncomfortable, not only for you but also for the rest of the siblings in your family. Your parents need to have a family meeting to lay down the rules of the home and how to settle conflicts. And you need to read the verse above and ask God to help you stop this quarreling and be patient with this situation. You will not be able to do this alone. You need to have God intervene in bringing peace to your family.

Questions to ponder:

What do you and your siblings fight about?

Discuss your last two fights and how they were resolved.

Be patient and humble with your siblings.

JOURNAL: _____

_____

_____

_____

_____

_____

_____

_____

_____

_____

_____

_____

_____

_____

_____

_____

_____

_____

_____

_____

_____

DEALING WITH STUBBORN FRIENDS

Q: I did something really dumb to one of my best friends. We were supposed to spend the evening together talking and doing girl stuff. But that day, a boy I really like asked me to go to the movies with him and his older brother. I was so excited that I said yes without thinking about my plans with my friend. So I called my friend and told her I wasn't feeling well and I wouldn't make it to her house. So I went to the movies with this boy in a group, and I couldn't believe my eyes when I saw my friend there with her parents. When she saw me, she shouted something and ran crying to the bathroom. I ran after her trying to apologize, but she wouldn't talk to me. I've tried to apologize to her every day, but even to this day (three weeks later), she won't speak to me. She is so stubborn about forgiving and forgetting.

What God Says: Matthew 18:15 *"If another believer sins against you, go privately and point out the offense. If the other person listens and confesses it, you have won that person back."*

A: Wow! Did you ever make a big mistake. You totally deceived your friend and got caught. The verse above applies to your friend. It would be great if she would go to you privately and express her hurt feelings and lack of trust to you. If she did, you could confess your mistake and apologize. However, in this case, you must be the aggressor and try whatever means to get her to talk to you. You can expect that she will continue to be stubborn because she is deeply hurt, but you must not give up when she shuns you. Go to God in prayer and ask Him for a miracle that your friend will have a change of heart. If you are truly sorry in your heart and it shows, then God will help you mend this friendship in His timing.

Questions to ponder:

How do you handle friends who are stubborn about things?

Do you try to help them? How?

> Don't live with a stubborn heart.

JOURNAL: _____

_____

_____

_____

_____

_____

_____

_____

_____

_____

_____

_____

_____

_____

_____

_____

_____

_____

_____

_____

_____

_____

_____

_____

_____

COMFORTING A SAD FRIEND

Q: My friend had a charm bracelet that she loved very much. She loved it mostly because her grandmother, on her death bed, gave it to her before she passed away. My friend wore the bracelet all the time, even when she was asleep. One day, she was changing for PE at school, and she accidentally left the bracelet on the bench in the girls' locker room. When she came back to change into her regular clothes, she noticed that the bracelet was missing. She asked everybody if they saw it, but no one did. She goes to lost and found every day, but no one has turned it in. She has been so sad since that day, and I don't know how best to console her.

> **What God Says:** Psalm 37:5 *"Commit everything you do to the LORD. Trust him, and he will help you."*

A: It is so difficult when we lose an item of priceless value because there is no way to replace it. Buying an identical charm bracelet will not have the same value as the one given to your friend by her grandmother. You need to continue to console your friend by just being there so she can have someone to cry with. But read the verse above, give this sad situation to God, and trust Him to make it better. God may not bring the bracelet back to your friend, but He will comfort her. The old saying that time heals all wounds is not necessarily correct. It is more accurate to say that God heals all wounds, for God created time to help us live with a loss. So again, encourage your friend to trust in Him, and He will be her strength.

Questions to ponder:

What would you do if you were the friend in this story?

How would you comfort this person?

> With God, s-a-d is just two letters
> from being g-l-a-d.

JOURNAL: _____

_____

_____

_____

_____

_____

_____

_____

_____

_____

_____

_____

_____

_____

_____

_____

_____

_____

_____

_____

_____

_____

_____

PROBLEMS WITH THE LAW

Q: My brother is a good kid who got caught up with a bad group. Every week, he goes to church, and sometimes he helps out in the toddler classroom. Now, there's this group of guys who go to his school and hang out on our street. These guys are thugs, but my brother liked them and wanted to be part of them because they got a lot of attention from girls. They knew my brother went to church, and they also knew that he wanted to join the group. So they told him that if he would steal all the cash in the offering bag and bring it back to them, he was in. See, my brother knew where they stored the cash after the offering was taken. He knew it was wrong, but the temptation was just too great, so he did it. Unfortunately for him, someone saw him, and he got caught. Now, he has a record and a bad reputation, and he's still not part of the group.

What God Says: Proverbs 1:10 *"If sinners entice you, turn your back on them!"*

A: Stealing is a hideous sin, but stealing from God's house is especially horrible. Your brother put more value on this group than he did on the sanctity of God's house. In my opinion, it's worse than just a bad reputation and a criminal record. He has thoroughly disappointed God with his actions, and he got nothing to show for it. God says to turn your back on those who want you to do evil. Walk away from the temptation and don't turn around, because it will only lead you to misery. Your brother must turn to God and ask him for forgiveness for his crime and then confess it openly to the church and make retribution (pay all the money back). Then he needs to vow never to do anything that irresponsible again. God is forgiving, and he will forgive your brother if he asks with his heart.

Questions to ponder:

Have you ever been in trouble with the law?
How about your family?
How about your friends or anyone you know?
Explain in detail.

Pray to God to deliver you from evil.

JOURNAL:_____

_____

_____

_____

_____

_____

_____

_____

_____

_____

_____

_____

_____

_____

_____

_____

_____

_____

_____

_____

_____

_____

_____

_____

OCTOBER 21

THREATS

Q: I was riding my bike after school toward home when I saw a car I recognized that belonged to my cousin. So I went looking around to see where he was. As I pulled up to a narrow alley, I saw my cousin standing there with four other guys. Then, I saw one of the guys hand my cousin a wad of cash, and my cousin handed the guy a baggie with drugs in it. He did the same thing with the other three guys. I really never realized that my cousin was a drug dealer. As I was leaving the alley, my bike hit a trash can and made a loud noise, which got my cousin's attention. At that point, he realized I knew what he was doing. That night, he came by my house and told me that if I said anything to the police or my family or anyone else, he would literally kill me!

What God Says: Psalm 121:7–8 *The Lord keeps you from all evil and preserves your life. The Lord keeps watch over you as you come and go, both now and forever.**

A: This is a terrible predicament to be in. You want to do the right thing as God teaches, but you also don't want to get physically hurt by your cousin. In situations like this, it is best to consult God's word where He tells us (like in the above verses) that He will keep us from evil and preserve our life if we trust Him. You need to go to God in prayer and ask Him for guidance in your situation. Listen to your heart, and God will provide an answer for you. My suggestion is to go to your parents or a pastor in confidence and ask for advice. God provides many answers for His people, and they can guide you in the right direction. And put your life in God's hands, and you will always feel safe.

Questions to ponder:
What would you do in this situation?

What do you think God would want you to do?

> God's strength is more powerful than human threats.

JOURNAL:

_____

_____

_____

_____

_____

_____

_____

_____

_____

_____

_____

_____

_____

_____

_____

_____

_____

_____

_____

_____

_____

_____

WASTING TIME, DOING NOTHING

Q: It was the first day of middle school, and the activities for that semester were posted for anyone to join. So my friends and I went to the board to see if there was anything good to sign up for. There must have been over 100 activities we could be involved in. One of my friends asked me to join band with him, but I refused. Another one asked me about cross-country running, but I said no. One by one, my friends were signing up for a couple activities each, but I kept saying no to all of them. By the end of the day, I hadn't signed up for anything. I figured I would just go home after school and play video games, watch TV, play with the dog, or just do nothing.

What God Says: Ecclesiastes 11:6 *Be sure to stay busy and plant a variety of crops, for you never know which ones will grow, and perhaps they all will.**

A: It sounds like you had an opportunity to be involved in numerous organizations, clubs, or sports and decided to do nothing. God teaches us in the verse above to experience as many good things as possible because we don't know which ones we have abilities for or which ones will help us grow in our lives. God works in mysterious ways through people or school activities, and what we may think is dumb or boring may turn out to be the best thing that has ever happened to us. But you will never know if you decide to waste your time away by doing nothing. God hates the idea of us wasting precious time because we are taking God's blessings and throwing them away. So get involved in good, positive activities that bring glory to God.

Questions to ponder:

What activities are you involved in?

What do you think of kids who waste their time?

Do you know kids like that?

Explain.

Opportunity missed is an opportunity lost.

JOURNAL:_____

_____

_____

_____

_____

_____

_____

_____

_____

_____

_____

_____

_____

_____

_____

_____

_____

_____

_____

_____

_____

_____

HELPING A FRIEND THROUGH TRIALS

Q: My friend and I were at a department store looking at all the different shades of lipstick. As we were leaving, a security guard stopped my friend to ask her to open her purse. He saw a brand new lipstick at the bottom of her purse. The guard accused her of shoplifting and told her to go with him upstairs so he could call the police. My friend is a good, honest person, and I know she didn't steal the lipstick. But they handcuffed her and escorted her to the escalator to take her to the waiting room. She was so humiliated. People were staring at her and pointing at her as though she were a common criminal. I didn't know how to help her in this horrendous trial.

What God Says: 1 Peter 4:12–13 *Dear friends, don't be surprised at the fiery trials you are going through as if something strange were happening to you. Instead be very glad because these trials will make you partners with Christ in His suffering, and afterward, you will have the wonderful joy of sharing His glory when it is displayed to all the world.**

A: This may not sound right, but God likes to see us on trial because it gives us an opportunity to put all our faith in Him. Think about this: If your life were perfect and you had no problems, no trials, no tough choices, and everything was just right, then why would you need God in your life? You would feel indestructible, needing no one. But we all know that life is certainly not like that. As the above verses say, trials allow us to be partners with Christ and trust Him to get through any situation. Have your friend put her trust in God so the truth can come out and she will be proved innocent and her good name restored. This is the time for her to run to God to help her through her trial.

Questions to ponder:

If this happened to you, what would you do?

If you knew you were innocent, how would you feel? Explain.

God rejoices when you turn to Him in your time of trials.

JOURNAL:

_____

_____

_____

_____

_____

_____

_____

_____

_____

_____

_____

_____

_____

_____

_____

_____

_____

_____

_____

_____

_____

_____

DISAPPOINTMENT

Q: My little sister is really good at gymnastics. From the time she was four years old until now (she's eight), I was her helper and biggest supporter. I never enjoyed gymnastics, but I saw how good she was and got excited for her. Well, last week, she had a gymnastics competition for six- to eight-year-old girls. I was sure she would win at least one event, maybe two or three. It turned out that she didn't win any of the events and only placed in one event (3rd place in the floor exercise). She wasn't too upset, but I was really disappointed at the whole thing. I thought the judging was unfair and that she didn't perform as well as she should. It's been a week, and I'm still feeling a little disappointed over the results of that competition.

What God Says: Nehemiah 8:10 *"Don't be dejected and sad, for the joy of the LORD is your strength."*

A: I think it's wonderful that you have taken such an interest in your sister's gymnastics. While most siblings fight, it's nice to see two sisters who love and support each other. The problem with judged sports like figure skating or gymnastics is that no matter how well you do, it is still up to someone else to decide a winner. You're not in control of the outcome. And often we walk away feeling cheated by the judging. But God says not to be sad and to turn to the Lord for strength and healing. There will be many more days ahead and tons of future gymnastic meets for your sister. One minor setback is nothing as long as she puts her faith in God and continues to train hard.

Questions to ponder:

When was the last time something disappointed you?

How did you handle it?

Losing is always disappointing, but God can lift our spirits.

JOURNAL: _____

_____

_____

_____

_____

_____

_____

_____

_____

_____

_____

_____

_____

_____

_____

_____

_____

_____

_____

_____

DEALING WITH FRIENDS WHO WON'T ADMIT THEY ARE WRONG

Q: Have you ever had a friend who never admits they're wrong? Even when you prove they are wrong, they won't admit it. I have a friend just like that, and he never admits to anything. And it's over the dumbest things like when we were talking about the 2003 Super Bowl and I told him that Tampa Bay beat Oakland. He kept telling me that Oakland won, and when I proved to him that he was wrong, he still wouldn't admit his error. It doesn't matter what the subject is or what the outcome might be, right or wrong, in his mind he's always right and everybody else is always wrong. It gets to the point that talking to him is extremely annoying.

> **What God Says:** Hosea 5:15 *Then I will return to My place until they admit their guilt and look to Me for help.**

A: People feel that admitting they're wrong is a sign of weakness. Actually, admitting you're wrong is a sign of maturity and wisdom. God often speaks in the Bible about admitting our faults and confessing our wrongs to others. Until we admit our failures and mistakes, how can we ask for forgiveness? Admitting our failures or faults is a true sign of humility. Unfortunately, people are just too proud to be humbled. As the above verse says, God wants us to admit when we're wrong, because until we do, He can't forgive us. It is extremely annoying to be around someone who always thinks they're right, even when you prove them wrong.

Questions to ponder:

How do you deal with friends who won't admit they're wrong?

Do you have friends like that?

Admitting failure is not a sign of weakness.

JOURNAL:_____

_____

_____

_____

_____

_____

_____

_____

_____

_____

_____

_____

_____

_____

_____

_____

_____

_____

_____

_____

_____

_____

_____

ARGUING

Q: I argue with my sister over the dumbest things. We argue over hair and make-up and which guy is cuter. We argue about who's doing chores and who's going to walk the dogs. We argue a lot about what time to get up in the morning to use the bathroom because we have only one bathroom for both of us. We argue a lot about food and what to make for dinner and who will make it and who will clean up after dinner. One of the biggest things we argue about is music. I like rock and roll, and she likes country western. So we argue about which one is better. We also argue about money and lending each other cash when the other one is broke. We argue about the silliest things 24/7, and I do wish it would stop.

What God Says: 2 Timothy 2:23 *"Again I say, don't get involved in foolish, ignorant arguments that only start fights."*

A: What a total waste of precious time to argue over such petty things when it's truly unnecessary. The answer to every argument is compromise, and in this case, that's what's needed. Set a schedule for chores so you'll know who does what and when. We all have different tastes in hair, makeup, and guys, so both of you can agree that your opinions are different and then move on. Regarding music, both rock and roll and country western are good, depending on your own taste in music. You'll see that you can begin to agree with each other on everything as long as you agree to compromise. God wants us to live in peace, and arguing over foolish things is not wise. Learn from God's teachings, don't get involved in ignorant arguments, and learn to compromise.

Questions to ponder:

Do you like to argue? Why or why not?

How often do you argue with your siblings or friends at school?

There is a compromise for every argument.

JOURNAL: _____

_____

_____

_____

_____

_____

_____

_____

_____

_____

_____

_____

_____

_____

_____

_____

_____

_____

_____

_____

_____

_____

_____

_____

_____

DEALING WITH A BITTER FRIEND

Q: My friend had this wonderful idea about how she could win a horse race that happened last weekend. She's an accomplished rider and has a secret method to get her horse to jump higher and run faster. She made the mistake of telling these secrets to a mutual friend. This mutual friend betrayed my friend's trust and told her biggest rival all the secrets my friend had told her. So at the meet, the rival used these secrets and beat my friend's horse by less than one second to win first place. After the race, the rival told my friend, "Thanks for the tips" and proceeded to tell her all the secrets that the mutual friend had told her. My friend was extremely angry and bitter, vowing never to speak to this mutual friend ever again and saying that she will hate her forever.

> **What God Says:** Proverbs 14:10 *"Each heart knows its own bitterness, and no one else can fully share its joy."*

A: What the verse above means is that your friend's heart will never experience joy until she gets rid of the bitterness. What your mutual friend did was wrong, and once a trust is broken, it is extremely difficult to mend it. But that's where God can help. We saw how betrayal worked in the life of Judas Iscariot who was one of Jesus's 12 apostles. Jesus treated Judas like a brother and treated him the same as all the other apostles. But for 30 pieces of silver, Judas betrayed Jesus and got Him arrested and ultimately crucified. But Jesus never hated Judas or expressed bitterness toward him. As we try to live our lives like Jesus, we must forgive our brothers and sisters and not be bitter. We cannot love others if there is bitterness in our hearts.

Questions to ponder:

How have you helped someone who is bitter?

Did it work?

What do you say or do to help stop the bitterness of friends or family?

Bitterness makes you feel hatred and anger inside.

JOURNAL:_____

_____

_____

_____

_____

_____

_____

_____

_____

_____

_____

_____

_____

_____

_____

_____

_____

_____

_____

_____

_____

_____

HELPING KIDS WHO ARE GREEDY

Q: Why are some kids in this world so greedy? They have everything they need in life, and yet they still want more and are never satisfied. That is a perfect description of this one kid at school. He comes from an upper-middle-class family who is rich compared to the rest of us. But if someone comes to school with a cool backpack or lunch box, he wants it, even though the one he has is brand-new. On a much simpler scale, if he has three or four pencils but I happen to have a mechanical pencil, he wants my pencil in spite of what he already has. He's a spoiled brat kid who only wants more and gives little. That's probably why he has such few friends.

What God Says: 1 John 3:17 *If anyone has enough money to live well and sees a brother or sister in need and refuses to help, how can God's love be in that person?**

A: Greediness is a terrible sin because it treats money and things of this world like something we can worship. Generous giving away of some of our material things is the most effective way to keep us from being greedy. You see, when we see what giving does in the life of other people, we experience a satisfaction that material things can never give. Greediness is the direct opposite of sharing, and those who always want can never be the same person who always gives. The end of your story shows what happens to greedy people. They usually have few friends because they don't know how to give. What is better, having fewer things but lots of friends who love you or having a ton of things and very few people who love you? It seems to me that the first one beats the second one every time.

Questions to ponder:
Do you know greedy kids? How do you deal with them?
If no, how would you deal with greedy kids?

Don't be greedy with your material things.

JOURNAL:

_____

_____

_____

_____

_____

_____

_____

_____

_____

_____

_____

_____

_____

_____

_____

_____

_____

_____

_____

_____

_____

_____

LIKING THE SAME BOY OR GIRL

Q: What do you do when two ninth-grade boys like the same eighth-grade girl, and she likes only one of them? That's the problem my best friend and I have with this one girl at school. She must be the hottest girl in the entire eighth grade, and my friend and I talk about her all the time. Well, the other day, I was talking to her in my science class (my friend is not in the same science class), and some kids overheard her telling me that she really likes me and wanted my phone number. I was thrilled until word got around to my best friend that she liked me. He started to act differently toward me. It was like he was jealous, although he kept denying it. Even to this day, our friendship has never been the same.

> **What God Says:** 1 Samuel 18:9–11 *Saul kept a jealous eye on David. A tormenting spirit from God overwhelmed Saul, and he began to rave like a mad man. Saul had a spear in his hand and suddenly hurled it at David intending to pin him to the wall. But David jumped aside and escaped.**

A: When two friends like the same girl (or boy), it usually ends up like this. No matter how good of friends you are, one usually ends up jealous of the other, which leads to a friendship deteriorating. In the verses above, both Saul and David did not like the same woman, but we can see what happens when we get jealous of someone. It leads to envy, then anger, then retaliation, and ultimately evil. God teaches us not to be jealous of anything. There are many hot girls (or cute guys for you girls out there), so there is no reason to be jealous over one. Always remember that boyfriends or girlfriends may last only a short while, but a true friendship can last a lifetime.

Question to ponder:

What would you do if you liked the same boy or girl as your best friend? Has that ever happened to you?

Don't choose a girlfriend or boyfriend over a true friend.

JOURNAL:

_____

_____

_____

_____

_____

_____

_____

_____

_____

_____

_____

_____

_____

_____

_____

_____

_____

_____

_____

_____

_____

_____

_____

DEALING WITH FRIENDS WHO TALK LOUDLY

Q: My good friend has a deep, powerful voice. He talks in a tone like an adult, but he's only in the eighth grade. The problem is that he can't control how loud he is. Even when it's just the two of us and we're talking right next to each other, he can be heard from far away. I've told him many times how loud he is, but he says he can't help it. It's really embarrassing if we are talking about something personal or about a girl. Everybody who is close by can hear everything he says, and sometimes we get teased or rumors start flying about our conversation. He is a really good friend and we have a lot of fun together, but I don't think I can take his loud voice anymore.

What God Says: Isaiah 32:17 *And his righteousness will bring peace. Quietness and confidence will fill the land forever.**

A: There are many instances where speaking in a loud voice is acceptable to people and to God. Singing songs of praise and preaching His word is wonderful in God's ears, no matter how loud they are. If your heart is filled with the Holy Spirit, then sometimes you just need to shout out your devotion to God. But other times, a loud voice can become irritating. God teaches us that a quiet, soft confidence with a subtle voice brings peace to all. So He urges us to speak softly but from the heart so our words have meaning instead of just loud noise. Regarding your friend, have him try to speak in a whisper when he talks to you, and when he gets excited and his tone rises, calmly ask him to whisper again. He may start getting used to talking with a lower tone. And through prayer and your help, he can hopefully reduce the loudness of his voice. Don't desert him as a friend; instead, support him in this effort to change this annoying habit.

Questions to ponder:

Do any of your friends talk loudly?

Do they sometimes embarrass you?

How do you handle it?

Use a loud voice to praise God.

JOURNAL:

_____

_____

_____

_____

_____

_____

_____

_____

_____

_____

_____

_____

_____

_____

_____

_____

_____

_____

_____

_____

_____

_____

_____

_____

_____

OCTOBER 31

QUITTING

Q: I've been in a church choir for about three years. It's kind of unusual for a ninth-grade boy to be involved in a church choir, but I like church and I love to sing, so it's a natural fit. The problem is that I get teased a lot for singing with all the girls. In our junior high choir, there are 10 girls and no boys. So I sing bass. I've had my fellow church guy friends tease me about this, and one of them told my next-door neighbor who went around telling everybody in the neighborhood that I sing in an all-girl choir. Now all the kids on my block laugh at me. So I decided to quit the choir. I don't want to constantly be treated like a goof.

What God Says: 2 Timothy 4:7 *"I have fought a good fight, I have finished the race, and I have remained faithful."*

A: God is proud of those who are faithful to Him no matter the cost. If the cost is money, material things, pride, or even accepting insults, God wants us to use our talents to glorify Him. He is thrilled when people endure for His sake. God blessed you with a good singing voice, and you used that talent to praise Him in the church choir. But as God has said many times in the Bible, including the above verse, it's not how you begin the race but how you endure it through all the hardships in life. And unfortunately, you decided to give in to the devil's work and quit singing in God's house. Do you think God was pleased with that decision? Probably not, but God is caring, loving, and forgiving and hopes you reconsider your decision. Don't allow the devil to win this fight. Go back to the choir and honor Him with your voice.

Questions to ponder:

Have you ever quit in ministry?

If yes, why?

If no, is there any reason why you would quit ministry work?

Explain!

Don't quit praising God. He will not quit on you.

JOURNAL:_____

_____

_____

_____

_____

_____

_____

_____

_____

_____

_____

_____

_____

_____

_____

_____

_____

_____

_____

_____

_____

_____

_____

The life lessons I have learned this month are:

_____

_____

_____

_____

_____

_____

_____

_____

_____

_____

_____

_____

_____

_____

_____

_____

_____

_____

_____

_____

_____

NOVEMBER 1

HELPING FRIENDS DEAL WITH ANGER

Q: My good friend at karate has a problem dealing with her next-door neighbor. He is constantly doing things to make her upset. First, he has a foul mouth, and every word is a cuss word. Then, he treats his kid brother like garbage, insulting him and being mean to him so loud that the whole neighborhood can hear. He throws his trash over my friend's fence just to get her angry. His 13-year-old buddies are always hanging out in her yard, and they sometimes sit on her grass just to annoy her. My friend and this neighbor boy have argued many times at his house or over the fence, but nothing changes. She is getting so angry at this situation that I'm afraid her neighbor might do something evil in the future. How can I help her in this situation?

What God Says: Psalm 37:8–9 *"Stop being angry! Turn from your rage! . . . For the wicked will be destroyed, but those who trust in the LORD will possess the land."*

A: I don't understand why this neighbor kid is acting so strangely. Does he have parents? Have you spoken to them about this situation? It is tough because we can't choose our neighbors, and sometimes we get stuck with bad ones. God teaches us to be kind and patient with difficult people. That doesn't mean to let them walk all over you. It means to carry yourself with a gentle and humble spirit but still try to fix the problem. First, you may need to set up a meeting with your friend, her parents, the neighbor, and his parents to hopefully come up with a positive solution to this problem. If that fails, then videotape his evil actions and show his parents to prove that what you are saying is true. If nothing works, you may want to consider moving to a better neighborhood.

Questions to ponder:

Do you have friends who get angry a lot?

How do you deal with them?

What normally calms them down?

Handle conflicts with kindness and gentleness.

JOURNAL:

CHANGING BEHAVIOR

Q: I treat my stepbrother badly, and I really need to change my behavior. He's not a terrible kid for a stepbrother, but sometimes he annoys me, and I blow things out of proportion. Like one day, I caught him spying on me, so I took his skateboard and tossed it in a dumpster. Or another time, he was bugging me so badly that I took apart his bicycle and hid some of the parts so no one could put it back together. One other time, I tied his arms to his bed during the night so he couldn't get up to use the bathroom, and he wet the bed. I thought they were harmless pranks, but I could see later that they really hurt him. That's when I realized that my behavior needed to change, especially toward him.

> **What God Says:** 1 Samuel 10:6 *"At that time, the Spirit of the LORD will come powerfully upon you, and you will prophesy with them. You will be changed into a different person."*

A: The first step to any recovery or attempt to change your behavior is to first recognize that you have a problem and want to fix it. So it looks like you've accomplished that. Next, you need to remove the evil from your heart and accept the spirit of God into your heart. You do that with a sincere prayer and asking God to take over your life. Last, you must make a conscious effort to be more Christlike in dealing with your stepbrother. Before doing something to him that is evil, ask God if He would be pleased with that action. Then, proceed with your heart and watch your behavior change, not only toward your stepbrother but toward everyone, for the spirit of the Lord will be with you.

Questions to ponder:

Is there a person in your life whom you treat badly? Who is it, and why do you treat them badly?

If no, what part of your personality do you need to change?

> To change your behavior, you need
> to change your heart.

JOURNAL:

_____

_____

_____

_____

_____

_____

_____

_____

_____

_____

_____

_____

_____

_____

_____

_____

_____

_____

_____

_____

_____

NOVEMBER 3

COMFORTING KIDS WITH GRIEF

Q: I heard a terrible story about a kid in my class whose mom was killed at a bank by two robbers stealing cash. It was a Friday morning, and his mom went inside the bank to make a deposit. Two people came in with masks over their heads, showing their guns and demanding all the money in the bank. As they walked past his mom, they noticed her diamond wedding ring and told her to give it to them. When she refused (the ring was a priceless heirloom from her great-grandmother), the robber tried to force it off her finger, and the gun went off. The bullet went in her chest, and she died at the hospital that night. This kid was in shock and grieving uncontrollably. I would like to help him, but I don't know how.

> **What God Says:** 2 Corinthians 1:4 *"He comforts us in all our troubles so that we can comfort others. When they are troubled, we will be able to give them the same comfort God has given to us."*

A: One of the countless amazing things about God is that He is a tremendous example for all of us when it comes to comforting a grieving friend. God is the ultimate example of comfort, solace, and relief, and we can learn all these traits from the Bible through Jesus Christ. Jesus healed many who were sick and comforted those who were in distress. What you need to do is be there for your friend. You don't necessarily have to say or do anything. You just need to be there for anything, from physical things to emotional support. Losing his mom who was just an innocent bystander is extremely difficult to handle. So just be there to comfort him, and read the Bible to see how God tells us to help those who are grieving.

Questions to ponder:

What would you say to someone if they lost their mom or dad in a brutal death?

How would you try to comfort them?

Has that ever happened to you?

God is the ultimate source of comfort.

JOURNAL:

_____

_____

_____

_____

_____

_____

_____

_____

_____

_____

_____

_____

_____

_____

_____

_____

_____

_____

_____

_____

_____

_____

_____

_____

KIDS WITH GAY FEELINGS

Q: My good friend told me a secret the other day that utterly shocked me, and I don't know what to do. She made me swear not to tell anyone, and I didn't. Then, she proceeded to tell me she has lustful feelings for another girl in my class and doesn't know what to do about it. We are both in eighth grade and talk about boys all the time. The only difference is that I talk about kissing guys and being with them, and she never says those kind of things. She just smiles and goes along with it, but I never suspected she had gay feelings. That goes against everything I believe, but she is a good friend, and I want to help her.

What God Says: Leviticus 20:13 *The penalty for a homosexual act is death to both parties. They have committed a detestable act and are guilty of a capital offense.**

A: There is no confusion about God's position on homosexual or lesbian acts. He says they are wrong and need to be changed. God made man and woman to be joined together as husband and wife and become one. He did not create man to be with man or woman to be with woman. That is detestable in the eyes of God. The best way to help your friend is to get her counseling by a pastor or Christian counselor who can help her understand why God feels it is wrong and help steer her in the right direction. It is very important to get her this help immediately before her feelings become too strong. But tell her that God always loves her no matter what!

Questions to ponder:

If your best friend thought he or she was gay, what would you do?

Would you try to help your friend? How?

Seek God when you are confused about your sexuality.

JOURNAL:

_____

_____

_____

_____

_____

_____

_____

_____

_____

_____

_____

_____

_____

_____

_____

_____

_____

_____

_____

_____

_____

_____

_____

_____

MOTIVATING THOSE KIDS WHO ARE UNMOTIVATED

Q: I am trying to motivate my brother to go out for the cross-country team. When he was in fifth and sixth grades, he had the fastest mile time in the class. As a matter of fact, his time was the best ever for that school. But now that he is in seventh grade, he says he's bored with running and would rather not go out for the team. He has the chance to be the best seventh-grade runner in the district, but even that doesn't motivate him. He's content just watching TV or playing video games. It upsets me that he has this wonderful talent but no motivation to excel. How can I change his lazy attitude?

What God Says: Proverbs 12:11 *Hard work means prosperity; only fools idle away their time.**

A: The problem is that you can't force someone to do something they don't want to do. On the other hand, nothing disgraces the father in heaven more than wasted talent. God gave that running talent to your brother. As the Bible says, to those who waste or hide their talents, no more will be given. He truly needs to stop wasting his time and use the skills God has given to him. You need to talk to him and find out the root reason for not wanting to run. He might have been pressured to run by your mom and dad. Whatever it is, find out what it is. And if it turns out that he doesn't run, then encourage him to find another activity he enjoys more and to do that. Don't waste this precious gift, because before we know it, time will be gone.

Questions to ponder:

Why is it important to not waste a talent?

What does God think of kids who are unmotivated?

Find your skill and do it.

JOURNAL:
_____

_____

_____

_____

_____

_____

_____

_____

_____

_____

_____

_____

_____

_____

_____

_____

_____

_____

_____

_____

_____

_____

_____

NOVEMBER 6

NO SENSE OF HUMOR

Q: I have really strict parents who have many rules I must follow. My dad is a Marine, and my mom is an ex-Army captain. They are very used to strict rules and regulations and no messing around. When both my parents are home, it is very serious with very little laughing and no joking. Unfortunately, that has caused me to have a limited sense of humor. At home, I'm treated like a soldier, so when I go to school, I have the same mindset, which is difficult to change. Kids tease me a lot for not having a sense of humor, but I don't know how to change it. It seems like I haven't laughed for a long time.

What God Says: Psalm 126:2 *We are filled with laughter, and we sing for joy.**

A: God loves for us to laugh. He created laughter and wants us to have joy and peace in our lives. The military is excellent for discipline, routine, and schedules, but not the best for laughter. When humor is lacking in a home, we sometimes need to go out and search for things to make us laugh. Go out today and rent a funny movie, buy a good joke book, or read a funny story. Bring things into your life that will make you laugh and have joy. Go to the circus or listen to a funny (and clean) comedian who helps you see laughter in a world full of anguish and sadness. Finally, learn to laugh at yourself. You'll find out that the best funny material around might be in the mirror.

Questions to ponder:
On a scale of 1 to 10, how would you rate your sense of humor?

Are there times when you can't take a joke? Why?

Don't rob your soul of laughter.

JOURNAL:

FRIENDS WITH PARENT PROBLEMS

Q: My friend doesn't treat his parents very nicely. His parents were born in Russia and came to the US about 15 years ago. They both have passive personalities and have a hard time disciplining their son. Well, my friend sure takes advantage of it. I've heard him yelling at his mom when something doesn't go his way. He has sworn at his dad many times, especially when it involved homework or chores around the house. He is always being sassy with both parents and shows them no respect. I know it's none of my business, but it bothers me the way he treats them. I wish he would treat them better and with more respect!

<u>**What God Says:**</u> Ephesians 6:3 *This is the promise: if you honor your father and mother, you will live a long life full of blessing.**

A: The least that God expects in the way we treat our parents is to show them honor, respect, and obedience. We already know that we'll never see eye-to-eye with our parents and that our opinions will differ on most things. But because of them, you were brought into this world, and for that alone, they deserve your love and respect. Your friend showing disrespect by swearing and yelling at his parents is detestable in the eyes of God. You need to lead by example. Show him how you treat your parents. Show him the love, honor, and obedience you give them, and hopefully, he'll learn the proper way to treat his parents. If he does that, he will be blessed by God.

Questions to ponder:
Are there things your parents do that make you angry?

List three things they do that anger you.

How do you try to cope with it?

Your parents deserve your honor and respect.

JOURNAL:_____

_____

_____

_____

_____

_____

_____

_____

_____

_____

_____

_____

_____

_____

_____

_____

_____

_____

_____

_____

_____

_____

_____

_____

HELPING KIDS WHO ARE OBSESSED

Q: My girlfriend is only happy when people are talking about her. She loves any attention she can get. It doesn't matter if it's positive or negative attention as long as people are talking about her. For example, one day she paid a florist to send flowers to herself on her birthday and told everyone they came from a guy from another school. Everyone was talking about her and those beautiful flowers. One day she came to school with pants so tight that the school sent her home to change. But again, she was the talk of the school. This girl is obsessed with attention, and she needs some serious help.

> **What God Says:** Galatians 1:10 *Obviously, I'm not trying to be a people pleaser. No, I am trying to please God. If I were still trying to please people, I would not be Christ's servant.**

A: Obsession is a compulsive, often unreasonable idea or emotion excessive in degree and nature. That sums up your friend's behavior. The need for that much attention usually stems from the lack of attention or acceptance at home. Going out of your way for positive or negative attention is a sickness that needs to be cured. She needs to focus all that energy of giving herself attention to giving God glory. She has the right idea, but she's doing it completely wrong. Encourage your friend to give her attention to God, and be a Christ-pleaser, not a people-pleaser. She will be blessed immensely, and she will feel so much better about herself.

Questions to ponder:

Do you know kids who crave attention?

How do you deal with them?

Be obsessed with being a Christ-pleaser.

JOURNAL:

REBELLIOUS KIDS

Q: There were a bunch of kids at my middle school who staged a mini-revolt against the school cafeteria. For years, students have been asking for different types of foods like pizza and crisp chicken, but all they serve is salad, liver, corned beef hash, and other stuff like that. So some of the more rebellious kids staged a strike against the cafeteria food being served. They did not allow anyone to eat at the cafeteria while they carried signs and banners against the food. After two days, the principal and his administrators got together and suspended all the kids who started the revolt, but they also had a PTA meeting to discuss the issue. So although the rebellious kids got suspended, their voices were heard. I'm just not sure it was really worth it.

What God Says: 1 Samuel 12:15 *"If you rebel against the LORD's commands and refuse to listen to him, then his hand will be as heavy upon you as it was upon your ancestors."*

A: There is a major difference between voicing your opinion on an issue (freedom of speech) and acting irrationally and irresponsibly (mini-revolt). God asks this question: What would you do if you did not like the Ten Commandments? Or how about the two main commands to love God with all your heart, soul, and mind and your neighbor as yourself? Will you rebel against God and not listen to Him? The point is that it is okay for kids to state their opinion, but it is not okay to act upon it in the wrong way. In other words, don't rebel against something you don't like but voice your view with love and gentleness. It's perfectly okay to disagree, but it is not okay to rebel in anger just because your requests are not granted.

Questions to ponder:

Do you know of kids who always want to rebel against authority?

What do you think of that type of kid?

Do you struggle with rules and authority?

> Don't rebel against God's commands, for the penalty is death.

JOURNAL:

_____

_____

_____

_____

_____

_____

_____

_____

_____

_____

_____

_____

_____

_____

_____

_____

_____

_____

_____

_____

_____

PRIDE

Q: We had a big science project due at the end of the month. I have to admit that I am one of the smartest students in the class. I always get A's on my tests and quizzes, and kids always want to study with me before a test. But for whatever reason, I was really struggling on this project. I couldn't find the right topic for my project. I researched a number of different things, but nothing seemed challenging or interesting. The other problem is that I had too much pride to ask the teacher or any of the other kids for help. See, I was supposed to be the smartest kid in this class, so I would look dumb if I looked like I needed help on this project. My pride got the best of me, and because of it, I only got a C on the project.

> **What God Says:** Proverbs 29:23 *"Pride ends in humiliation, while humility brings honor."*

A: Normally, the result of anything in which pride plays a part is similar to your situation. Most people do not understand the power of pride. It can destroy everything in a person's life, including themselves. The best way to turn pride into humility is to always remember that everything you have (intelligence, material things, abilities, talents, etc.) belongs to God, and He gave them to you as gifts for being His child. You did nothing to deserve those gifts, but God gave them to you anyway because He loves you. Once you totally believe that, then pride will turn into humility and gratitude to God for what He has done for you. And as the verse says, humility leads to honor, and that is pleasing to God.

Questions to ponder:

Do you have a lot of pride?

If yes, what do you have pride in and why?

If no, how do you keep your pride in check?

Turn your pride into humility.

JOURNAL:_____

_____

_____

_____

_____

_____

_____

_____

_____

_____

_____

_____

_____

_____

_____

_____

_____

_____

_____

_____

_____

_____

_____

_____

HELPING A FRIEND WHO WANTS TO RUN AWAY

Q: My friend has a very large family. There are two parents, eight kids, and three grandkids all living under the same roof. My friend's oldest sister just recently divorced her husband and moved back home with her three kids. So, there are 13 people in a four-bedroom, two-bathroom home. My friend hardly ever gets to talk to his parents because they are so busy working and taking care of the rest of the family. He feels totally ignored and unloved by his family and gets no attention from anyone. He knows that if he ran away from home, no one would notice. He told me one day that he is planning to run away just to see if his parents will try to find him.

What God Says: Isaiah 40:31 *But those who wait on the Lord will find new strength. They will fly high on wings like eagles. They will run and not grow weary. They will walk and not faint.** *

A: That sure is a lot of people in one house. I can see how someone could get lost in the shuffle with 13 people under one roof. Your friend is feeling lonely and abandoned by his family. He wants to run away so he can get some attention from his mom and dad. Although I feel for him, running away is not the answer. God teaches us to find courage and strength in difficult situations, and we need to turn to Him for guidance. He will help your friend get rid of the feeling of abandonment and renew His spirit in his heart. Without God, he'll be wandering around like a lost sheep. With God, he'll have renewed energy and hope for the future. Tell your friend not to run away but to run toward God, and He will save him.

Questions to ponder:

What would you advise a kid who wanted to run away for good reason?
Do you have any friends in a similar situation?

If you need to run, run toward God.

JOURNAL:

RISK

Q: There was this group of high school kids who were picking on my sister. There must have been about 10 of them harassing her and trying to steal her money and do other mean things. My sister is in the sixth grade, and I'm only in the ninth grade, but I'm pretty big for my age. I got sick and tired of hearing my sister cry over these punks, so I decided to take a risk and do something about it. I followed my sister to her school, and this group of high school kids started to harass her again. Without thinking of the danger, I ran up to the biggest kid in the group and challenged that punk to back off. I'm not sure why, but all the kids started to back down and walk away. And since that time, they haven't bothered my sister.

What God Says: Joshua 1:7 *Be strong and very courageous. Obey all the laws Moses gave you. Do not turn away from them, and you will be successful in everything you do.**

A: It took a lot of guts for you to do what you did to help your sister. You risked getting hurt to help someone in need. That is the definition of a hero. A hero is someone who puts another person's needs ahead of their own to save that person. I commend you on your courage. But most kids would not have taken the same risks that you did. They would have been too afraid of getting hurt. God can help those who are scared but want to do the right thing. He tells us in the verse above to be strong and courageous and live by His laws, and you will have success. He tells us to turn to Him for strength in times of adversity. When you need to take a risk to help God's children, remember that you are never alone. God will always be there at your side.

Questions to ponder:

Honestly, would you have stood up to those high school kids to protect your little sister?

If not, what would you have done?

Living your life for God is no risk.

JOURNAL:

_____

_____

_____

_____

_____

_____

_____

_____

_____

_____

_____

_____

_____

_____

_____

_____

_____

_____

_____

_____

_____

_____

_____

_____

_____

SHOWING FRIENDS HOW TO SAY NO TO OTHERS

Q: My friend's parents are really cool. We have a lot of fun over there listening to music, dancing, and eating junk food. They don't have a lot of rules, but one is real important to them. They set curfew at 10:00 p.m. with no exceptions. They feel that's late enough for a 14-year-old girl. Well one night, we all went to the movies, and it got out at 9:45 p.m. The rest of the group and I wanted to get a pizza afterward. My friend saw the time and knew it was close to curfew, but she really wanted to go with the group. We were all putting pressure on her to go, but she told us all no, that she had to be home by 10:00 p.m. She showed all of us, including me, how to say no to others.

> **What God Says:** Genesis 39:10–12 *She kept putting pressure on him day after day, but he refused to sleep with her, and he kept out of her way as much as possible. . . . She came and grabbed him by the shirt. Joseph ran out of the house.**

A: The greatest example in the Bible of saying no to someone when the pressure was great is the story of Joseph (Gen. 39). Joseph was in charge of Potiphar's household. Potiphar was the captain of the Egyptian palace guard. But Joseph was very handsome, and Potiphar's wife wanted to have sex with him. It would have been very easy for Joseph to secretly have sex with this beautiful woman while Potiphar was away, but he knew it was wrong, so he declined her advancements. This led to the verse above where Joseph continued to say no to her. Let this be an example of how you should live your life. When you know something is wrong, you need the courage to do the right thing. It may be tough, but God can help you through it if you ask Him. Your friend did the right thing by obeying her parents' rule, so she should feel proud.

Questions to ponder:

In all honesty, would you have gone home by 10:00 p.m. to meet curfew, or would you have gone with your friends to get pizza?

Why or why not?

Has this ever happened to you?

Say no to wrong; say yes to God.

JOURNAL:

_____

_____

_____

_____

_____

_____

_____

_____

_____

_____

_____

_____

_____

_____

_____

_____

_____

_____

_____

_____

_____

_____

_____

TERMINAL ILLNESS

Q: Just last year, I was diagnosed with muscular dystrophy. I could not understand why I wasn't growing like the other kids, and my muscles were not strong. When I went to the doctor, no one could figure out the problem at first. No one suspected muscular dystrophy because it is usually detected in much younger kids. But one doctor diagnosed it after running numerous tests for a type of muscular dystrophy called limb-girdle. This form of muscular dystrophy affects mostly the hips and shoulders. He says I'll probably be confined to a wheelchair when I'm 15 or 16 (I'm 13 now) and I could die before I reach 30 years old. I'm very scared and a little upset with God for why He allowed this to happen to me.

> **What God Says:** Psalm 41:3 *The Lord nurses them when they are sick and eases the pain and discomfort.**

A: Anyone in your situation with your circumstances would be very scared. And there is nothing wrong with being upset with God because you are only human. But in time and as quickly as possible, you need to turn that anger toward God to love for Him. God did not cause you to get this terrible disease. He did not get up one day and say, "I'm going to give you a muscle disease because I just feel like it." Unfortunately, terrible things happen to good people in this world. But like the old saying goes, life is 1% what happens to you and 99% how you react to it. You need to turn to God for help to ease your pain and give you strength to endure the rough days ahead. God promises to ease the discomfort of those who are sick but trust in His love.

Questions to ponder:

Do you blame God when things go wrong in your life?

If yes, give an example.

If no, whom do you blame?

Don't blame God for your illnesses.

JOURNAL:

SEXUAL THOUGHTS

Q: I have a problem. I have sexual thoughts about girls all the time. I'm not talking about *Playboy* pictures or pornography. I'm talking about girls in my class, girls on my street, and girls at the mall who I'm physically attracted to. I start fantasizing about being with them and making out and doing other intimate acts. I'm not sure how I got this way. Like I said, I don't look at naked magazines, rent X-rated movies, or look at naked women on the Internet (my dad has it blocked, anyway). But these thoughts are constantly going through my mind, and I don't know how to control them. I'm only 13 years old, and I haven't even kissed a girl yet.

What God Says: 1 Thessalonians 4:3–4 *God wants you to be holy, so you should stay clear of sexual sin. Then each of you will control your body and live in holiness and honor—not in lustful passion as the pagans do in their ignorance of God and His ways.**

A: I'm just wondering how these sexual thoughts get into your head if you're not looking at naked women in movies, the Internet, or magazines. You must have an active imagination after seeing love scenes or romantic moments on TV. Whatever it is, you do need to control it before you do something later on that you might regret. Your mind is a powerful tool that God has given you. We have the power to fill our minds with whatever subjects we want. Right now, you need to make a conscious effort to free your mind of all sexual thoughts and control your brain with more pure, godly thoughts. Pray to God for help to think thoughts of good and wonderful things and not lustful passion.

Questions to ponder:
Do you have sexual thoughts all the time?
If yes, how are you controlling them?
If no, what do you think about most of the time?

> You can control your mind with God's help.

JOURNAL:

_____

_____

_____

_____

_____

_____

_____

_____

_____

_____

_____

_____

_____

_____

_____

_____

_____

_____

_____

_____

_____

_____

_____

NOVEMBER 16

DEALING WITH A PERSON CONTEMPLATING SUICIDE

Q: I am really worried about a good friend of mine who lives on my street. When I first met her, she was always sad. Then, I found out later from her parents that she suffers from severe depression. She is on a medication that keeps her positive and happy, but when it wears off, she can get manic-depression. Well, just last week, she found out that her parents are separating and moving away from each other. One is moving 1,500 miles away, and the other is moving 3,000 miles away. My friend loves living here, and she loves her friends and school. After she found this out, she threw her medication down the toilet and hasn't taken it for seven days. Her mom says she is extremely depressed and all she wants to do is die. We are all worried that she will commit suicide.

> **What God Says:** Jeremiah 29:11 *"'I know the plans I have for you,' says the LORD. 'They are plans for good and not for disaster, to give you a future and a hope.'"*

A: In a nutshell, God did not create your friend so she can destroy herself. It would be no different if I created a beautiful picture for you, made with my own hands, and then you totally destroy it. How do you think that would make me feel? That is how God feels about suicide. And if your friend turns her life over to God, there will not be a reason to want to commit suicide. You see, it doesn't matter what your circumstances, your depression, or your problems are; God has a solution for you. All you need to do is ask Him for deep spiritual strength and read His word for guidance and help. Tell your friend that and have her see a Christian counselor or pastor. Please tell her not to waste this beautiful gift God has given her. The gift of life is a precious thing to waste. God loves her unconditionally and forever.

Questions to ponder:

What would you do or say to this kid in the story to change her outlook on life?

Has anyone you know ever thought of suicide?

Don't ever destroy what God has created.

JOURNAL:
_____

_____

_____

_____

_____

_____

_____

_____

_____

_____

_____

_____

_____

_____

_____

_____

_____

_____

_____

_____

_____

_____

NOVEMBER 17

HELPING A FRIEND WHO CAN'T TRUST

Q: My friend's sister is in high school (eleventh grade), and my friend and I are in middle school (ninth grade). It's the type of school where the middle school and the high school share the same campus, separated only by a fence. There's this one boy that my friend has liked for months, and a couple months ago, he asked her to be his girlfriend. My friend was so excited that she told everybody—her parents, her friends, and her sister. She said it was the happiest day of her life. Last week, we were standing outside the school fence when we saw my friend's boyfriend kissing her sister. It seems that her boyfriend only asked her out to get a chance to go out with her sister. Her sister knew how much she liked him but was making out with him anyway. My friend says she'll never trust her sister again.

> **What God Says:** Psalm 118:8 *It is better to trust the Lord than to put confidence in people.**

A: One of the toughest acts to forgive is when someone betrays a trust or friendship to fulfill their own desires. In this case, two people betrayed your friend's trust: her sister and her new boyfriend. God wants us to forgive all those who hurt us, but it is so hard to forgive a broken trust. Your friend is extremely hurt, and it will be difficult for her to trust again. That's why God says it is better to trust Him than put your trust in people. God will never abandon you, lie to you, hurt you, or be mean to you, and you can trust Him in everything. But in this situation, your friend needs to turn to God and ask for wisdom and strength to deal with her sister and her ex-boyfriend.

Questions to ponder:

How would you comfort a friend who has been betrayed by his or her own family?

How would you help him or her trust again?

Trust God and put your confidence in Him.

JOURNAL:

DEALING WITH ARROGANT KIDS

Q: How do you deal with someone who is really arrogant and cocky, so much that it makes you sick to your stomach? In our school, each kid gets teamed up with a desk partner, and they work together throughout the semester on a variety projects and experiments. Unfortunately, I got teamed up with this kid who is extremely arrogant about everything. When we're playing during lunch, he's just a big show-off. When we're doing a project together, he has to show how smart he is, but all he does is run his mouth and do nothing. He's a first-class, arrogant jerk, and I have to put up with him for an entire semester. What can I do?

What God Says: Micah 6:8 *The Lord has already told you what is good, and this is what He requires: to do what is right, to love mercy, and to walk humbly with your God.**

A: A person who is arrogant is basically someone who feels they are more important than they actually are. In their own minds, arrogant people think they are better than everyone else. Usually, people who are important and talented don't need to be arrogant because other people already recognize their value. It is those who hear nothing from others who feel the need to toot their own horns. Most arrogant kids have few friends because they feel they don't need anybody. All you can do with this kid is be around him as little as possible, only when necessary. God sums up for us how we are to live our lives: do what is right with mercy and humility. Continue to live with God and with your many friends, and maybe this kid will get the hint about how to become a humbler person.

Questions to ponder:
Who do you know who is arrogant?
How do you deal with them?
Do you struggle with arrogance?

You can't walk with God if you are self-absorbed.

JOURNAL:

_____

_____

_____

_____

_____

_____

_____

_____

_____

_____

_____

_____

_____

_____

_____

_____

_____

_____

_____

_____

ADVISING GOOD KIDS WITH BAD INTENTIONS

Q: My friend has a stepbrother, and the two of them don't get along at all. If you've heard of opposites, it's these two guys. My friend loves all sports and is very athletic. His stepbrother hates sports and enjoys drawing and music. They fight all the time about everything; even I get tired hearing it, and I'm only over at his house once a week. This upcoming weekend, his stepbrother has a competition for drawing and painting. My friend has been praying to God that his stepbrother will do poorly; his intention is for God to hear his prayer and not help his stepbrother win. He also planned to rip up his stepbrother's picture for the contest, but I stopped him from doing that. My friend is a good kid but with terrible feelings for his stepbrother.

What God Says: James 4:3 *When you ask, you don't get it because your whole motive is wrong—you want only what will give you pleasure.**

A: Unfortunately for your friend, God will not answer prayers that have intentions for evil to others. God is all about love and compassion and not about evil and hate. God will always say no to any prayer requests with bad intentions. These two brothers need to stop acting badly toward each other and start treating each other with love and respect. I see a ton of deadly sins with these two brothers, starting with jealousy and selfishness and, most of all, hatred. They need to turn to the Lord to help them change their bad feelings for each other. Have them start looking for the good qualities in each other instead of the negative. Once they start communicating positively, it will open the doors of their hearts, changing from evil to good. Then you won't have to be concerned about your friend having bad intentions with his brother. But remember, it all starts with God.

Questions to ponder:

What advice would you give this kid who wants to ruin his stepbrother's drawing for a competition?

Do you ever pray for evil on another person?

Don't pray for bad will against others.

JOURNAL:

HELPING FRIENDS WHO NEED TO BE COOL

Q: Sometimes, I have a hard time understanding why kids my age have this tremendous need to be cool. I have friends who would do anything to be considered cool by other kids. Let me give you an example: In our school, leather jackets are considered cool (don't ask me why). Those who wear leather jackets are considered bad, so to keep up with this reputation, they do evil things. Well, my friend really wanted to be cool, but he couldn't afford a real leather jacket. These cool kids told him to just go ahead and take money from his mom's purse when she wasn't looking until he had enough to buy a jacket. Sure enough, he did it and got his leather jacket. Now my friend is allowed to hang out with this cool group, and he's starting to act just like them. I just don't understand why.

> **What God Says:** 3 John 11 *"Dear friend, don't let this bad example influence you. Follow only what is good. Remember that those who do good prove that they are God's children, and those who do evil prove that they do not know God."*

A: The reason kids need to be cool is because they want to be accepted by their peers. And being accepted by your peers usually requires you to do something that is crazy or mean to show your toughness. And in our society, toughness is cool. Since God is all about goodness, kindness, and love, it is not considered cool to act like Jesus at school. God teaches us to follow good examples that lead to positive things in life. When you follow evil and malicious behavior, the devil thinks you are cool. When you follow what is right and show love to others, God is well pleased. And whom would we rather please?

Questions to ponder:
How far would you go to be accepted as cool?
Give examples of things you've done to be cool.
How did it work out for you?

Be cool with God and not the devil.

JOURNAL:

_____

_____

_____

_____

_____

_____

_____

_____

_____

_____

_____

_____

_____

_____

_____

_____

_____

_____

_____

_____

_____

_____

NOVEMBER 21

EVIL THOUGHTS FROM OTHERS

Q: There's a girl on my block, and I'm convinced she is possessed by the devil. The things she says and does are just downright evil. Nothing comes out of her mouth that isn't mean or nasty. I built up my nerve to ask her why she is so negative. She told me that only evil thoughts go through her head, and that's the way she is. I don't think this girl has a compassionate bone in her body. She once told my friend that she hates cats and that the next time she sees one, she will catch it and cut its head off. That is the way her mind thinks. She's very violent in her thoughts and deeds, and I'm afraid that one day she will snap, bring a weapon on campus, and kill some innocent people.

What God Says: 1 John 2:15 *Stop loving this evil world and all it has to offer.**

A: To most people, sin often appears lovely, attractive, and cool. The thought of doing evil makes us feel tough and makes people afraid of us. Thinking evil thoughts and doing evil things are a terrible habit that we know is wrong and bad for us. But like this girl, once you have a reputation for evil, it is difficult to break the thought process. The only way to stop a bad habit of thinking evil is to replace it with good, positive thoughts. That can only be accomplished with the help of God. God is all good, and if this girl asks Him from her heart, He will hear her and change her evil thoughts to something good. Any of us could act like this girl if we allow evil to penetrate our hearts and souls. We all need to stop conforming to evil thoughts in this world and allow God to mold our hearts for good.

Questions to ponder:

Do you know someone like this girl in the story?

As a Christian, how would you try to help her change her thoughts?

Only God has the power to change evil to good.

JOURNAL:

_____

_____

_____

_____

_____

_____

_____

_____

_____

_____

_____

_____

_____

_____

_____

_____

_____

_____

_____

_____

_____

_____

HEAVEN

Q: I think I know now how to get to heaven (January 13) and what I would look like in heaven (June 22), but who actually goes to heaven? Is it only church people, or do people who don't go to church but are nice to everyone go to heaven as well? How about little kids who die at a young age? Do they go to heaven? My cousin has never set foot in a church in his life, but he would do anything to help anyone. He's always helping my dad with his car and problems with his house. He's always giving good advice to my sister, and he's very compassionate to others. But since he doesn't go to church, does that mean my wonderful cousin will not go to heaven?

What God Says: John 3:16 *God so loved this world that He gave His only son so everyone who believes in Him will not perish but have eternal life.**

A: The most famous verse in the Bible says it all. God sent His son in the name of Jesus Christ to this world to die on the cross so we can have eternal life with God. It is up to us to turn our lives and hearts over to Christ so we can live eternally in heaven. So what does that mean? It means we cannot get to heaven just by being nice and being a good person because we are all sinners, and God cannot have sinners in heaven. God sent His son to wash away our sins on the cross. What we need to do is accept Christ into our hearts for the forgiveness of our sins and follow His ways. The only way to heaven is through Christ, not through good works or being nice. When it comes to small children, God welcomes all children into heaven if they are too young to make the decision to be a follower of Christ.

Questions to ponder:

In your mind, who goes to heaven?

In your mind, what is needed for you to go to heaven?

What are your questions about heaven?

Invite Jesus into your heart for the pathway to heaven.

JOURNAL:

PRAYER

Q: I believe in prayer, and I think it's important to pray to God as often as possible. My problem is that I don't know what to pray for and how to ask God for things when He already knows what a terrible sinner I am. I can just picture God in heaven when I'm praying to Him. He probably looks at my past and present and then doesn't listen to me. Not that I can blame Him. I've only been on this earth for 14 years, but I've done enough sins to last a lifetime. Does God really hear the prayers of sinners like me? Or am I just wasting my time since I'm not worthy to ask God for anything?

What God Says: 2 Chronicles 7:14 *"If my people who are called by name will humble themselves and pray and seek my face and turn from their wicked ways, I will hear from heaven."*

A: God does not judge you when you pray. He doesn't say, "Well, since this person sinned many times last week, I won't listen to their prayer." God is merciful and full of grace, and He will forgive our sins if we ask Him with all our hearts. We must confess our sins and then pray in a way that we seek God with all our heart in a humble manner. Prayer is an expression of our intimate relationship with our father in heaven who loves us unconditionally. The verse above says it all. We must seek Him out and turn from our wicked sins. God will not only hear us, but he will help us get through this evil world. None of us are worthy of God's ear, but that's what makes God so awesome.

Questions to ponder:

Give an example of an answered prayer in your life.

Describe what you prayed for and for how long.

How often do you pray?

Pray with a humble and contrite heart.

JOURNAL:

ADVISING KIDS WHO WANT TO PIERCE THEIR BODIES

Q: A buddy of mine thinks that body piercing is real cool. He currently has one earring in each ear, but he wants so much more than that. My friend is only 13 years old, but he's planning to get a nose ring next. His problem is that his parents do not want him to get this nose ring, and they'll lecture him if he does. So he's thinking about a belly button ring first, and he can always wear shirts that cover it up, and his parents won't notice. But he says that as soon as he turns 18, he's definitely getting his eyebrows and tongue pierced, and that's just for starters. I think body piercing is awful, and I would like to talk him out of it, but I don't know how.

> **What God Says:** Romans 6:13 *Do not let any part of your body become a tool of wickedness to be used for sinning. . . . And use your whole body as a tool to do what is right for the glory of God.**

A: My personal opinion is that I don't understand why anyone would want to pierce any part of his or her body. It's got to hurt when it's being done, and I don't think it looks that cool. But different people have different tastes. All that really matters is what God thinks of piercing your body. We do know that back in the time of Moses, a pierced ear meant that a servant pledged his lifelong service to his master (Exod. 21:6). God has made it clear that our body is a temple, and piercing is scarring the body in the eyes of the Lord. Desecrating the body with piercing is like destroying a temple, and that is not pleasing to God. Our bodies belong to the Lord. We need to treat them with reverence and beauty. Don't pierce your body, because it destroys the beauty of what God created.

Questions to ponder:

What advice would you give a friend who wanted to pierce their body? Why?

Would you ever get a body piercing?

Your body belongs to God; do what He says is good.

JOURNAL:

_____

_____

_____

_____

_____

_____

_____

_____

_____

_____

_____

_____

_____

_____

_____

_____

_____

_____

_____

_____

_____

_____

_____

HELPING KIDS WHO WANT WHAT OTHER PEOPLE HAVE

Q: There is a rich kid in my school who has a pair of Nike high-top Air Jordan shoes and a Michael Jordan authentic jersey that he wears to school. There's a group of guys who really don't like this rich kid, but they really love his tennis shoes and jersey. So they got together and made a plan to jump him after school and steal his shoes and jersey. The problem is that word got out that this was going to happen, and somehow, the rich kid heard about it. So instead of going home his normal way, he got a ride from his older brother. That made this group of guys extremely angry that their evil plan leaked out. The rich kid never wore those tennis shoes or jersey to school again.

> **What God Says:** James 4:2 *You want what you don't have, so you scheme and kill to get it. You are jealous of what others have and can't possess it, so you fight and quarrel to take it away from them. And yet the reason you don't have what you want is that you don't ask God for it.**

A: There is a major difference between personal needs and personal wants. Wearing shoes to warm our feet is a need; wearing Air Jordan high-tops is a want. Wearing a shirt to warm your body is a need; wearing an authentic Jordan jersey is a want. God will always provide for our basic needs if we ask Him with a humble heart. But He won't necessarily give us our personal wants, especially when we ask for them in a sinful manner. Kids should be happy to have shoes and shirts because there are so many kids in this world who would be thrilled to have anything to cover their feet and bodies. The verse teaches us how God hates the act of coveting and making evil plans to take things from others. Remember to thank God for what you do have instead of wanting what other people have been blessed with.

Questions to ponder:

Make a list of five things you want. Have you prayed to God for them? Do you think God answers prayers for our wants?

Ask humbly for your needs, and you shall receive.

JOURNAL: _____

_____

_____

_____

_____

_____

_____

_____

_____

_____

_____

_____

_____

_____

_____

_____

_____

_____

_____

_____

_____

_____

_____

_____

NOVEMBER 26

COMFORTING KIDS WHO ARE DEEPLY DEPRESSED

Q: My friend's life is just falling apart. Just in the last month, she found out that her brother has cancer and her mom (who is the only provider) got laid off from her job. My friend is a pretty emotional person to begin with, but the shock of these two events has just about sent her over the edge. Since then, she rarely eats anything and hasn't slept much. Her grades, which are usually A's and B's, have been falling, and she has been absent from school three times in the last two weeks (not because of an illness). Way back when, she told me she gets deeply depressed when things start going wrong in her life, and I'm afraid that's what's happening now. She has no other family who lives close by. Her dad left their family and moved to another country. How can I help an emotion-filled girl through her deep depression?

> **What God Says:** 1 Corinthians 3:16–17 *Don't you realize that all of you together are the temple of God and that the spirit lives inside of you? God will bring ruin upon anyone who ruins His temple. For God's temple is holy, and you Christians are that temple.**

A: The verse is saying that how can anyone be deeply depressed if the spirit of God lives inside of you? The Holy Spirit is about love and joy and goodness and kindness, but not sadness and depression. Your friend needs to turn to God now and ask Him to strengthen her life. She needs to speak to a Christian counselor who can pump all the positive things about life into her head. She needs to get her attitude adjusted from hopelessness to hope, and the only way to accomplish that is with God through people here on earth. The worst thing a depressed person can do is isolate themselves against the world. Have her talk to strong Christian professionals soon to start changing her depression back to a life of Christ-centered joy.

Questions to ponder:
How would you help a friend who was deeply depressed?
What would you say?

Depression to joy may be just a prayer away.

JOURNAL:

NOVEMBER 27

GOOD JUDGMENT

Q: I am currently in the seventh grade, and we have a seventh-grade formal dance this coming weekend. I'm really excited about it even though no guy has asked me to it, but I'll still go with all my friends as a group. The problem is that one of the high school football players is having a party after the dance. There are supposed to be chaperones there, but this guy has a reputation for sneaking around doing drugs and drinking beer. I have a feeling that there will be alcohol there and a lot of drugs. My friends are excited about going to this party after the dance, but I'm not sure if it would be smart for me to go to a party that I'm sure will have alcohol and other illegal stuff. My heart wants to go, but my better judgment is telling me to just go to the dance and then go home.

> **What God Says:** Proverbs 14:2 *"Those who follow the right path fear the LORD; those who take the wrong path despise him."*

A: A lot of adults as well as kids struggle in this area of good judgment. Most of us make quick decisions, and they usually turn out wrong. Following the right path is not always the easiest thing to do. It is so much easier to follow the devil's path and make mistakes. You know in your mind and heart that you shouldn't go to the party after the dance since it will be weakly chaperoned with a lot of smoking and drinking. Saying yes is the easy decision but probably the wrong path. You need to use good judgment and not put yourself in a place of temptation when you know there's nothing but trouble lurking. Follow God's path and have fun at the dance, and then go home. You'll be glad about that decision in the long run.

Questions to ponder:

Do you normally use good judgment?

Give an example of when you used good or bad judgment.

Would you have gone to this party after the dance? Explain.

Strong will and character lead to good judgment.

JOURNAL:

DOUBTS ABOUT GOD

Q: I have been a Christian kid for as long as I can remember, thanks to my parents taking me to church every Sunday. I do believe in God, but sometimes I truly wonder how God can allow so much suffering in this world. You hear about the wars in the Middle East and the battles in Afghanistan. Where was God when all the innocent people died in the 9/11 destruction of the Twin Towers in New York? If God is so loving, so wonderful, so caring of all His people, then why does He allow these tragedies to happen? God is all-knowing even before terrible things happen like the World Trade Center disaster. Why can't He prevent all the destruction of innocent lives if He loves His people? It really gives me doubts about what God is all about.

> **What God Says:** Hebrews 13:5 *God has said, "I will never fail you. I will never forsake you."**

A: This question comes up a lot when talking about God. If He is a loving God, then why is there so much suffering in this world? Why do so many innocent people die? The main reason is because people have the freedom to choose what they want to do with their lives. If people want to kill, they have that choice. If people want to hurt innocent people, they have that choice. If we didn't have free choice, then we would all be God's robots or puppets with God programming us or pulling the strings. So all God can do is comfort the victims of other people's bad choices. Suffering also brings people closer to God. If everything were perfect with no pain and suffering, then why would we need God? How can God be part of our lives if we have no use for Him? Pain and suffering and killing and bombs are unfortunately part of our world today, but God is there to comfort us when we turn to Him. God is the comfort in the chaos!

Questions to ponder:
Why doesn't God intervene before a catastrophe like 9/11 happens?
Why can't God end the war in the Middle East?

God's comfort is greater than our suffering.

JOURNAL:

_____

_____

_____

_____

_____

_____

_____

_____

_____

_____

_____

_____

_____

_____

_____

_____

_____

_____

_____

_____

_____

_____

_____

_____

_____

KIDS WITH BIG EGOS

Q: There is a kid in my class whose dad is a professional baseball player. He's been playing major league ball for almost 10 years, and he's really good. What isn't good is that because his dad is well-known, this kid has a huge ego. He walks around school like he's king of the hill, and what's funny is that the kid is not really good at anything. It is truly annoying that this kid who has not accomplished a thing in his life gets treated better by some of the teachers and thinks he's all that because of what his dad does for a living. Most of the kids at school can't stand him because of his egotistical personality, and the ones who do tolerate him do so only to get free tickets to home games or merchandise or autographs.

> **What God Says:** 1 Peter 5:6 *Humble yourself under the mighty power of God and in good time, He will honor you.**

A: There is never a good reason for a person to have a big ego. But it is even worse when this ego comes from absolutely nothing. In other words, some people have big egos because they've accomplished something in life. But this kid has a famous dad and has accomplished nothing and still has a big ego. This kid has become so self-absorbed that he thinks he's worth more than he is. God loves the simple and humble and despises the boastful and egotistical. He will honor those who are humble and turn His back on those with big egos. And I would rather get my praise from God than from people any day.

Questions to ponder:

Do you know kids with big egos?

If yes, how do you handle them?

If no, how would you handle them?

E.G.O.: Earning God's Outrage.

JOURNAL: _____

_____

_____

_____

_____

_____

_____

_____

_____

_____

_____

_____

_____

_____

_____

_____

_____

_____

_____

_____

_____

_____

_____

_____

MAKING SMART CHOICES

Q: Do you know of someone who always seems to make the wrong choices in life? That perfectly describes my friend at school. He's a good kid with a good heart but not too smart in making choices. For example, he had a choice of watching a late-night movie or going to bed on time and being ready for a big test the next day. He chose watching the movie, and because he was exhausted, he failed the test. He had a choice of riding his bike to school on a potentially rainy day or getting a ride from his mom. He chose riding his bike, and sure enough, it poured down rain and he was sick for three days. He had a choice of practicing tennis for a big match or playing around with his friends. He chose playing around with his friends and lost the tennis match in the first round. I'm not sure why he always makes the wrong choices, but his life would be easier if he didn't.

What God Says: Proverbs 3:6 *Seek His will in all you do and He will direct your path.**

A: It sounds like your friend is not getting good advice or no advice at all when he's making decisions. Before making choices, it's always smart to get the opinions of others, either your parents, a trusted friend, or a brother or sister. Then you will have other ideas and points of view to help you make smart decisions. But the best way to make good choices is to go to God in prayer. Ask Him what the best choice is, and He will guide you in the right direction. Like the verse says, He will direct you down the right road to a smart choice. God wants to be your friend, and He wants to help you in your daily decisions, but you need to go to Him with an open mind and a humble heart.

Questions to ponder:

Do you seek God's word when making a choice?

If yes, has it helped you make smart choices?

In no, why not seek God first?

All smart choices begin and end with God.

JOURNAL:

_____

_____

_____

_____

_____

_____

_____

_____

_____

_____

_____

_____

_____

_____

_____

_____

_____

_____

_____

_____

_____

_____

_____

_____

The life lessons I have learned this month are:

_____

_____

_____

_____

_____

_____

_____

_____

_____

_____

_____

_____

_____

_____

_____

_____

_____

_____

_____

_____

_____

_____

_____

DECEMBER 1

BURDENS

Q: It seems like I'm going through a lot of problems in my ninth-grade year that I've never experienced before. I have big problems with my lower back that I hurt about four months ago in a skiing accident. It's getting progressively worse, and the doctors are puzzled about the next step to relieve my pain. I usually get A's in my classes, but this year, I'm struggling with C's. I'm also starting to have problems with my dog. He's eight years old, and all of a sudden, he stopped eating and being playful, and I don't know what's wrong with him. We took him to the vet, but they couldn't find any problems. It just seems like I'm overburdened right now with all these things, and they're really starting to get me down. I need something to lift my spirits and take some of these problems away.

> **What God Says:** Matthew 11:29-30 *Take My yoke upon you. Let Me teach you because I am humble and gentle, and you will find rest in your souls. For My yoke fits perfectly, and the burdens I give you are light.**

A: Well, you sure came to the right place because I've got the perfect solution for all your troubles. God is waiting with open arms to take away all your burdens and physical ailments and give you peace of mind. There is nothing else, no drug or medication or song or anything, that can relieve your burdens better than God. He promises that to us in the verse above when He says that you can find rest for your soul in Him. So you need to talk to God and ask Him to help you with your daily burdens, and then trust Him to relieve your emotional pain. God loves you very much, and He wants to carry your burdens for you if you will allow Him to.

Questions to ponder:
What do you do when you feel burdened?
Who do you turn to? Why?

God is the perfect medicine for the burdened soul.

JOURNAL:

DECEMBER 2

DRINKING AND DRUGS

Q: I can't believe the number of drugs and amount of alcohol there is at my high school. I see kids smoking pot before and after school in their cars and in the alleys. I heard of a kid who brought alcohol in a thermos and then poured soda in it to make his mixed drink. The teachers are aware that there is a problem, but because the high school is so large, there isn't a lot done to solve it. And the amount of pressure put on kids to be cool and get high or drunk is enormous. I tried to talk to my parents about it, but they don't believe me when I tell them how much drugs are at my school. I don't do drugs or drink at all, but the pressure to try it is enormous. How can I stay sober and drug-free yet still survive at this school?

What God Says: Ephesians 5:18 *Don't be drunk with wine, because that will ruin your life. Instead, let the Holy Spirit fill and control you.**

A: It is extremely discouraging to know there is so much drugs and alcohol in a high school. This is a choice you need to make. Do you fill your body with drugs and alcohol to get a quick buzz, or do you fill your body with the Holy Spirit to get an eternal high? If you allow the Holy Spirit in your life, it will help you fight off the temptations of drugs and alcohol. You need God's strength and power to not give in to the evils of this world and to let God control your path. Remember, God is much more powerful than the pressures of evil if you allow Him to fight with you against it.

Questions to ponder:
Are there a lot of drugs at your school?
How about alcohol?
How do you reduce the pressure to participate in drugs or alcohol?

Fill your body with the Holy Spirit.

JOURNAL:

DECEMBER 3

HELPING KIDS AT A NEW SCHOOL

Q: Last week at our school, we had a new kid start who just moved from across the country. It was the end of the first quarter, and boy, did he ever look scared. He had no idea where he was going or what his classes were. He had no friends, and he knew no one, so he was totally alone. A couple of the kids took advantage of that and "accidentally" knocked his books over. One kid told him the wrong directions to his classroom. I felt sorry for this guy, but I didn't know what to do. I didn't want to look like a nerd and help him because I would get teased, but I knew he really needed a friend. What can I do to keep my reputation intact and yet help this new kid feel welcomed?

> **What God Says:** Psalm 46:1 *God is our refuge and strength, always ready to help in times of uncertainty.**

A: In today's world, it is not popular to help out someone in need. You are looked upon as weak or strange, especially if you are a boy. You know that God would want you to help this kid and be his friend. The best way to accomplish that and yet not lose your reputation is to take him aside (just the two of you) and tell him that you want to help him and be his friend. Invite him to your house and, in time, introduce him to your buddies. Once he starts fitting in with the other kids and they see he's a cool person, then he'll start becoming more comfortable at school. Also, pray for God to be with you and give you the strength to make this first move to befriend this kid. Remember, doing a nice deed for this kid is the same as doing it for God.

Questions to ponder:

How do you treat new kids at your school? Explain.

Why do you think kids are so mean to new kids?

God is proud when we deny ourselves to help others.

JOURNAL: _____

_____

_____

_____

_____

_____

_____

_____

_____

_____

_____

_____

_____

_____

_____

_____

_____

_____

_____

_____

_____

_____

_____

_____

_____

LONELINESS

Q: Let me describe my situation: I'm 13 years old, and I'm on the volleyball team—one of the best players. I get good grades at school and get along with just about everybody. My parents are very supportive of me, and I have one brother and one sister whom I love. I have a group of close friends that I normally hang out with during the day. Despite all these positive things in my life, most of the time, I feel so lonely that I could just die. I have no idea what it is, but when I'm at home or at school or at volleyball games, I feel so alone, even though I'm around other people. It feels like something is missing in my life, but I don't know what.

What God Says: Psalm 23:4 *Even when you walk through the dark valley of death, you are close beside Me.**

A: It sounds like something is missing in your life. You seem happy, and you are doing the right things, but there is no joy. It sounds like you are looking for a purpose in life to make it more meaningful. The only way I know to gather purpose for life is through God. It is God who gives our life meaning and understanding about why we were put here on earth—that is, to serve Him. You need to get involved in Christian activities that serve God through other people. Then, you will get that feeling of worth. Also, keep in mind that when you are feeling alone, you never really are because God is with you. He will take away that feeling of loneliness if you let Him.

Questions to ponder:

Are you ever lonely in a crowded room?

If yes, how do you deal with it?

If no, how would you handle it?

With God, you are never alone.

JOURNAL:_____

_____
_____
_____
_____
_____
_____
_____
_____
_____
_____
_____
_____
_____
_____
_____
_____
_____
_____
_____
_____
_____
_____
_____
_____
_____
_____

DECEMBER 5

INSINCERE KIDS

Q: Do you know kids who look so sweet and nice and humble on the outside, but after you get to know them, they're mean and insincere? That's the situation with this one girl in my class. Everybody just seems to love her. The girls think she's great; the guys want to date her because she is so nice and pretty. We became better friends, and I got to know the real person. She speaks so highly of God and the Bible and praying, but I found out that she never goes to church. As a matter of fact, when it was just the two of us, she told me that she hates church and that God is not part of her life. In front of a crowd, she's an angel. But behind their backs, she gossips about people and spreads mean rumors. She's as insincere as it gets.

What God Says: James 1:26 *"If you claim to be religious but don't control your tongue, you are fooling yourself, and your religion is worthless."*

A: This girl has the look of an angel but the heart of the devil. This type of person puts on a good show to impress people with their good spirit and righteousness only to get praise. God teaches us that no matter how many people are fooled by our acting, God knows our hearts. He knows if our words and devotion toward Him are superficial and worthless. She may be able to fool some, but she'll never be able to fool God. Maybe you can talk to her in a humble way, point out that what she's doing is wrong, and help her change to a truly nice person.

Questions to ponder:

What do you think of kids who are nice on the outside but not on the inside? Do you know anyone like that? Explain.

> Be true and sincere with everyone.

JOURNAL:_____

_____
_____
_____
_____
_____
_____
_____
_____
_____
_____
_____
_____
_____
_____
_____
_____
_____
_____
_____
_____
_____
_____
_____
_____
_____
_____

DECEMBER 6

HELPING FRIENDS WHO FEEL BAD ABOUT THEMSELVES

Q: I have a problem medically when it comes to being clumsy. The doctors say it's a coordination problem, and for whatever reason, even though I'm in the seventh grade, my motor skills do not function properly. There is nothing wrong with my mind or my body, just my motor skills. That means there are times that I miss my mouth when I'm eating, or I'll just fall down for no reason when I'm walking. I bump into things and knock things down, not on purpose, but I can't help it. Needless to say, I get teased unmercifully at school and on my street. I get called names all the time like goof and a joke and moron. I really feel bad about myself. I may be stupid and a moron, and maybe the kids are right that I'm a goof.

> **What God Says:** Deuteronomy 26:18 *"The Lord has declared today that you are his people, his own special treasure."*

A: No, you are not any of those things. You are a child of God, and He loves you tremendously. God knows of your medical condition and does not care that you bump into things or spill your food or drink. He cares about your heart and how you are serving Him. You need to believe that God treasures you like a prized possession and that He's there to protect you. So you need to pray to God to help you control your coordination problem or at least give you strength and confidence to put up with these rude, uncaring kids who call you names. Kids can be mean, and you can't control that, but with God at your side, you can better fight this battle and definitely not feel bad about yourself. See yourself as God sees you: a treasure!

Questions to ponder:
Do you tease kids who act strange?

Why or why not?

You are a priceless treasure in the eyes of God.

JOURNAL:

GLUTTONY

Q: I have a terrible eating disorder. I absolutely love food and desire it 24/7. Here's a typical day of eating for me. I have breakfast in the morning, usually cereal, toast, bacon, and orange juice. At my first break at school, I have a snack like a cupcake or donut. At second break, I have another snack, usually a bag of chips. Then at lunch, I buy two or three slices of pizza, hamburgers, or burritos, along with more chips and a drink. At third break, I have another snack (usually pudding or candy). When I get home from school, my mom fixes me another snack before dinner, and then I have a full meal at dinner. Finally, around 8:00 p.m., I have dessert. I have gained almost 60 pounds this year, and I can't stop eating. If I don't stop soon, I just might blow up!

> **What God Says:** Proverbs 23:20–21 *Do not carouse with drunkards and gluttons, for they are on their way to poverty.**

A: To God, gluttony is a sin because it is the opposite of self-control, a gift from the Holy Spirit. But from what you describe, you have a serious medical problem of overeating, and you need to be careful. You need to find a substitute for food. It sounds like when you are happy, you turn to food; when you are sad, you turn to food. No matter what the situation or the emotion is, you turn to food. Why don't you try turning to God instead when you have the urge for food? Fill up your mind and soul with the food of God's word, and allow that to be the source that fills you. By doing this, you'll lose a lot of weight and not be obsessed with eating, and you'll be gaining valuable wisdom while serving God. You can't beat that combination!

Questions to ponder:

When you have a problem, where do you turn—friends, food, or family?
Do you turn to the Bible?
Give specific examples.

Gluttony is the opposite of self-control.

JOURNAL: _____

_____

_____

_____

_____

_____

_____

_____

_____

_____

_____

_____

_____

_____

_____

_____

_____

_____

_____

_____

_____

_____

_____

_____

_____

DECEMBER 8

KIDS WHO DESPISE FOR NO REASON

Q: I go to a large high school with a lot of different ethnic groups around campus. We have African Americans, Hispanics, Asians, and Middle Easterners. Most of the time, these kids hang out with their own nationality. There is a group of Hispanic boys who, for whatever reason, totally despise the Asian kids. The Asian kids have done nothing to the Hispanic kids, never called them names or racial slurs or been disrespectful. But they just don't like them. It may be that the Asian boys get better grades, or maybe because they excel in the martial arts. What I don't understand is how one group can hate another group for absolutely no reason. They may look different and talk different, but they are all people and should be respected.

What God Says: Romans 5:5 *God has given us the Holy Spirit to fill our hearts with love.**

A: Some kids just despise others for the sheer love of hating. They just don't like anybody who is different from them. Or some kids just hate because they don't know how to love. They have never been shown any love or attention, so they don't know how to give it. These kids would learn how to love if someone showed them what love is. They all hang out together because that is the closest to brotherly love they are going to get. It's just too bad that their sole purpose is to despise others rather than love one another. It would be great if these kids could learn about God. God is love, and when we accept Him, He sends the Holy Spirit into our lives so we can love others. Maybe you know of a youth pastor or worker who has had an experience like this and has found that God can talk to these Hispanic kids in their language about the value of love and about God.

Questions to ponder:

Do you know kids of one ethnic group who hate others from a different nationality or culture?

Does it bother you?

How do you deal with them?

Don't despise anyone; love one another.

JOURNAL:_____

_____

_____

_____

_____

_____

_____

_____

_____

_____

_____

_____

_____

_____

_____

_____

_____

_____

_____

_____

_____

_____

_____

_____

DECEMBER 9

HELPING KIDS WHO FEEL LIKE FAILURES

Q: I have a friend who seems to struggle at everything he does. He has tried out for basketball and track but did not make either team. He tried out for a school play, but since he couldn't memorize his lines, he did not get the part. He tried playing a musical instrument but didn't like it very much, so he failed at that, too. Unfortunately, he's not one of the best students in the class. He struggles getting Cs and Ds on his report card even though he studies real hard. He has this feeling once in a while that he is a complete failure and not good at anything. I want to help his low morale, but I don't know what to say because he fails at everything.

> **What God Says:** Psalm 37:23–24 *The steps of the godly are directed by the Lord. He delights in every detail of their lives. Though they stumble, they will not fall, for the Lord holds them by the hand.* *

A: Believe it or not, God could care less if this friend of yours can play sports or a musical instrument or if he can memorize lines or get good grades. God looks at success and failure by how we serve Him and whether we are using our talents to glorify Him. If we fail in all aspects of life but live our lives for Christ and serve others, then God sees us as a tremendous success. How we measure success and how God measures success are totally different. God doesn't care what grades we get or how much money we have or what kind of car we drive. He cares about our hearts and what we do in our lives for His people. So do you want people or God to decide if you are a success or a failure? Please let your friend know.

Questions to ponder:

What would you say to a friend who feels like a failure?

How would you encourage him or her?

Do you have a favorite verse to share?

To God, we only fail if we don't trust Him.

JOURNAL:_____

_____

_____

_____

_____

_____

_____

_____

_____

_____

_____

_____

_____

_____

_____

_____

_____

_____

_____

_____

_____

_____

_____

LAZINESS

Q: I've been in karate for about two years, and I had a goal of becoming a black belt before my 15th birthday. I was a purple belt, so all I needed was brown, then red, and then black. If I trained at least twice a week for the next two years, I should have been able to make it. Then all of a sudden, my attitude started to change. I got lazy and did not want to go to the dojo twice a week. And when I was there, I didn't give 100% effort. I only went through the motions. I started getting lazy in other things as well, like homework and chores around the house. Needless to say, I did not get my black belt by my 15th birthday. Because of my laziness, I'm still a purple belt.

What God Says: Proverbs 15:19 *A lazy person has trouble all through life.**

A: Laziness is a terrible sin because it takes a precious gift from God called time and throws it out the window. Laziness accomplishes nothing, and it only disappoints the people who love us, and it disappoints us. Read the verse above again and see what God thinks about lazy people. If you are lazy now, how are you going to be as you get older? You will probably be the same, and as God says, you will have trouble throughout your life. Make a stand now and stop being lazy. Get yourself into things that will please your father in heaven. Go get that black belt now, or if you've lost interest in karate, then find something else. And with whatever you choose, always, always give your best effort, because God expects no less.

Questions to ponder:

Has laziness ever cost you a medal, a trophy, or any other honor?

If yes, explain the circumstance.

If no, how do you prevent laziness?

Lazy kids usually turn into lazy adults.

JOURNAL:

DECEMBER 11

HOW TO DEAL WITH A CHATTERBOX

Q: I've got a friend who just can't stop talking. If we are talking on the phone, she talks 90% of the time, and I can barely get a word in. Even when we are in a group of friends, she dominates the conversation. And she talks about everything and everybody. She loves to gossip about other people. She spreads rumors about kids, but it's never verified. She talks mean about kids she doesn't like. She even makes up stories, like the one time she told us about her trip to Hawaii and how great it was and how awesome the beaches were. I found out from her older sister that she has never been to Hawaii. She's a good friend, but her worthless and lying chatter is getting on my nerves.

What God Says: 1 Peter 3:10 *The Scripture says, If you want a happy life and good days, keep your tongue from speaking evil and keep your lips from telling lies.**

A: Kids who speak many words but say nothing are fools in the eyes of the Lord. It's one thing to say a lot of nothing; it's totally another thing to speak lies and evil about others. That goes totally against what God instructs, and He promises an unhappy life and bad days ahead. Does your friend realize what she is doing? There are people who talk and talk and talk and don't realize they are dominating a conversation. They need to be told to think more and speak less so their words have some meaning. Otherwise, when she does have something important to say, people will not listen to her and will ignore her. Make all your spoken words count, and don't use your tongue as a weapon to speak evil or speak lies.

Questions to ponder:
How would you deal with a kid who never stops talking?
Is it annoying?
Do you know anyone like this?
Explain.

A tongue can pierce hearts like a sword.

JOURNAL:

DECEMBER 12

HOW TO DEAL WITH FRIENDS BECOMING ENEMIES

Q: My buddies and I decided to repair bikes and restore skateboards for money. We thought it would be a good way to make some extra cash over the summer for Christmas or whatever. Each of us had a job to do. My buddy would advertise and bring in the business. I would do all the work on the bikes and skateboards, and my other friend would collect and handle all the money. Everything was going really well until something did not seem right. We were doing a lot of business, but we weren't seeing a lot of the money. We found out that the friend who was handling the money was pocketing about 70% of the profits and giving me and my other friend the other 30%. It didn't bother me a lot, but my advertising buddy was mad. He didn't want anything to do with my other friend, and he told me they were enemies for life because of his stealing.

What God Says: Luke 6:27–28 *I say, love your enemies. Do good to those who hate you. Pray for the happiness of those who curse you. Pray for those who hurt you.**

A: Your friend who took the money betrayed the friendship with you and your other friend, and betrayals are very difficult to fix. Still, the Lord teaches to love our enemies and do good to those you don't like or have harmed you. That doesn't mean you need to love what they did to you. Your friend needs to love your other friend as a person and a child of God but hate the dishonesty and betrayal. People sometimes get confused that we must love those who brutally hurt us. You continue to love the person and pray for them to change from the wickedness and turn to God. It is extremely tough to do that, but with God's help, it can be done. Forgiveness heals an angry heart.

Questions to ponder:
Has a friend ever betrayed you?
If yes, how did you handle it?
Have you ever betrayed a friend?

> You may hate his deeds, but you must love your neighbor.

JOURNAL:

FORGETFULNESS

Q: There isn't a day that goes by that I don't forget something when I'm going somewhere. If I'm going to school, I forget my homework assignment sheet or my lunch. If I'm coming home from school, I forget my books to study or my worksheets for homework, or even my backpack. If I'm going to soccer practice, I forget my soccer shoes or water bottle. It's not like I do it on purpose. Maybe it's because I have so many things on my mind that I forget the little things. My parents say it's irresponsibility; I say it's just forgetfulness.

What God Says: Deuteronomy 6:12 *"Be careful not to forget the LORD."*

A: God is concerned that if you forget the small things in life, you might forget the important things, namely Him. When it comes to the little things, you need to change your habits. It's silly to ever think that continuing to do things the same way is going to change the results. You need to learn to write things down or make a conscious effort to have a mental checklist of everything you need when you leave a place. For the important things in life, like worshipping God, you need to focus on that as important and set your priorities straight. If God is your number-one priority (and I pray He is), then He will always be at the top of your mind and will never be forgotten.

Questions to ponder:

Are you like this kid in the story?

If yes, how can you change your ways?

If no, how can you help others be less forgetful?

Change this bad habit of forgetfulness.

JOURNAL:

DEALING WITH FRIENDS WHO NAG

Q: I have a lot of friends at high school, but there is one girl who is such a nag. She comes from a strict family who enforces strict rules, so she brings that same type of attitude to school. If I'm chewing gum before school, she tells me I'm going to get in trouble. If I'm talking to someone else in class, she nags me. If I'm wearing a strapless top, she nags me. It's almost like having a second mother at school. She's a good, loyal friend, but her mothering me has to stop.

> **What God Says:** Numbers 14:27–29 *How long will this wicked nation complain about Me? I have heard everything the Israelites have been constantly saying. Now tell them this. Because you have complained against Me, none of you twenty years or older will enter the land I swore to give you.**

A: The role of a friend is to be there in time of need and love you for who you are. They are not there to nag. They are not your parents, who do have the responsibility to teach you right from wrong and discipline you when you make mistakes. There is also a big difference in praying to God and nagging Him. Praying to God means asking God from your heart for your wants and needs. Nagging God means demanding results from God and not waiting for His perfect timing, just like the Israelites did in the above verses. Tell your friend to stop nagging you. Advising you once for what is right is a good friend, but continued nagging is a nuisance.

Questions to ponder:

How do you handle friends who nag you all the time?

Are you a nag to your friends at times?

Be persistent and humble in prayer. Do not nag.

JOURNAL:

DECEMBER 15

HELPING FRIENDS WITH A GUILTY CONSCIENCE

Q: One day, my friend got real angry with his uncle. His uncle had promised to take him to the basketball game last month, and he never showed up. The following week, he promised to take him to the movies, and again, he didn't show up or call. Seems like he was working late or something, but he didn't have the decency to call. Then, last week, he swore he would take my friend to the circus. And without fail, he didn't show up or call. My friend was extremely angry, disappointed, and bitter at his uncle. So when he saw him the following week, he let him have it. He yelled at him. He cursed at him. He said many mean things to him, like he wished he was dead. The next day, he thought about what he said and started to feel guilty. He wanted to apologize, but he was still mad about what his uncle had done to him.

> **What God Says:** Romans 3:24 *God in His gracious kindness declares us not guilty. He has done this through Christ Jesus who has freed us by taking away our sins.**

A: Your friend was hurt and angry with his uncle. So he made a choice to unleash his anger at him. The anger was understandable, but his methods were wrong. He should have never spoken to his uncle when he was that angry. In most cases, we will say something or do something dumb that will make us feel guilty later on. He should have waited until he was calmer and then discussed his frustrations in a more rational voice. That way, his words would have meant more, and in the end, he wouldn't have had such a guilty conscience. Normally, doing it the right way will make the other person feel guilty for what they've done to you. Thanks to Jesus, all your friend needs to do to get rid of his guilt is first apologize to God for his sin and then apologize to his uncle for the way he talked to him. A sincere apology will ease any guilty feelings.

Questions to ponder:
How do you help friends with a guilty conscience?
What advice do you give them?
Name a time when you felt guilty for what you did or said.

A sincere apology is the medicine for a guilty conscience.

JOURNAL:

DECEMBER 16

CONTROLLING LUSTFUL THOUGHTS

Q: I think my friend has a problem. He's 13 years old and has been collecting *Playboy* magazines for about two years. He hides the magazines in the garage so his mom and dad won't see them. When I first heard about it, I thought it was kind of fun to look at adult magazines at our age. But I think my friend has gone a little overboard. He now subscribes to *Penthouse* magazine, and the other day, he told me he got hold of an X-rated movie and asked me if I wanted to watch it with him. He is constantly thinking about naked women and sexual thoughts. I'm afraid he might do something stupid like abuse a girl sexually or something worse. How can I help him?

What God Says: Matthew 5:28 *I say, anyone who even looks at a woman with lust in his eye has already committed adultery with her in his heart.**

A: Your friend seems to have active hormones, and you're right—his obsession for naked woman and pornography will lead him to trouble in the long run. It's one of those situations that the right thing to do would be to tell his parents what's going on so he will hopefully stop, but you don't want to betray his trust in you as a friend. But if a friend is heading in the wrong direction fast, it is always better to risk a friendship to save the person. Tell his parents to check your friend's hiding places as discreetly as possible and keep your name out of it. It doesn't matter how his parents find out as long as they do and then do something about it. God has strong words about lustful thoughts; it is as if you had sexual intercourse in your mind. Although your friend is obviously not committing adultery because he's not married, he is still committing a terrible sin that needs to stop.

Questions to ponder:

Do you agree that lustful thoughts could lead to sexual action?

Why or why not?

Do you struggle with lust?

How do you control it?

Lustful thoughts lead to sexual action.

JOURNAL:

DECEMBER 17

DEALING WITH UNFORGIVING FRIENDS

Q: My friend does not want to forgive me for falsely accusing her of taking money from my house. We were the only ones in the house one day, and my mom had left two $20 bills on the table. Well, we were upstairs listening to music and singing and laughing. A couple times, she went downstairs to get some chips. Later that evening, her mom picked her up, and I noticed the $40 missing from the table. Immediately, I began accusing my friend of stealing the cash when she came downstairs for chips. She denied it many times, but I kept accusing her. Turns out the next day that my mom told me she came home and grabbed the money to get a couple things at the store. We never heard her because the music upstairs was too loud. How can I get my friend to forgive me for accusing her of stealing the $40?

> **What God Says:** Colossians 3:13 *You must make allowances for each other's faults and forgive the person who offends you. Remember the Lord forgave you, so you must forgive others.**

A: You made the huge mistake that we all do of jumping to conclusions without having all the facts. You automatically assumed that your friend stole the money, and instead of asking her gently, you accused her, which tells her that you don't trust her. All you can do now is apologize sincerely and beg your friend to forgive you. That starts with God. Ask God to give you the wisdom and strength to approach your friend and ask her for forgiveness. Then ask God to open her heart to your humble plea and accept your apology. The best way to repair the friendship is to go back and do the things you enjoy doing together to make good memories. This will hopefully erase the bad memories of your accusations. If your friend loves the Lord, remind her that since God always forgives her sins, she needs to forgive others.

Questions to ponder:
Have you ever falsely accused a friend of wrongdoing?

If yes, how did you make up to them?

If no, how would you make up to them?

Always be humble when asking for forgiveness.

JOURNAL:

DECEMBER 18

HELPING FRIENDS WHO GET YELLED AT A LOT

Q: My friend's dad is a screamer. And boy, does he have a loud voice. He's a drill sergeant in the Army, and his job is yelling and screaming at the new recruits during boot camp. So sometimes, when he gets home, he forgets where he is and starts yelling the same way to my friend (his son). My friend hates it when he yells. It makes him feel useless and very sad. Sometimes, he just wants to lash back at his dad, but he knows he would be disciplined severely. So he's between a rock and a hard place. I really would like to help him, but I don't know how. If only his dad would treat him like a son and not a private, it would be so much better.

> **What God Says:** Ephesians 4:29 *Let everything you say be good and helpful so your words will be an encouragement to those who hear them.**

A: His dad needs to understand that his son is not a recruit in the Army but his child. I don't blame your friend for not liking it when his dad yells at him. I don't think anyone does. The only thing your friend can do is sit down with his dad and very respectfully tell him this issue. His dad probably doesn't even realize he's doing it. He is probably so used to screaming in boot camp that he forgets when he gets home. I'm pretty sure if your friend talks to him positively and from the heart, it will change his dad's way of talking to him. Have him show his dad the verse above. The only way his words can be an encouragement to his son is if they are spoken softly and positively. Let this verse be a lesson for any of us who yell and scream too much.

Questions to ponder:

How do you help friends who get yelled at a lot?

Do your parents scream at you?

What is your opinion of parents who yell at their kids?

People listen much better when the yelling stops.

JOURNAL:_____

_____

_____

_____

_____

_____

_____

_____

_____

_____

_____

_____

_____

_____

_____

_____

_____

_____

_____

_____

_____

_____

_____

_____

HELPING KIDS GET BACK ON TRACK WITH THEIR CHRISTIANITY

Q: I have one of those familiar stories of a good kid going bad. My friend and I have been attending the same church for three years. We were both Christian boys who loved God. But my friend wanted to be popular, so he abandoned the church and started hanging out with the cool group. All this group did was smoke cigarettes, get high, and fight with other kids. After being involved with this group for six months, he realized he wasn't really as happy as he was before and that he was acting dumb. So he decided to break away from this group. Now, he wants to go back to church with me, but he feels so bad about all the sins he's done in the last six months that he doesn't think God will accept him back. He wants to recommit to Christianity and make it stick this time, but he doesn't know how.

> **What God Says:** 2 Corinthians 5:17 *Those who become Christians become new persons. They are not the same anymore, for the old life is gone. A new life has begun.**

A: God will accept anyone back to Him as long as they repent, ask Him for forgiveness, and then give their life back to God. God is all about love, not hate or revenge or grudges. He wants us back in His light and will always accept us with open arms. Once we do this, we are back in fellowship with God. All our past sins are forgiven and forgotten by God. We are considered reborn through the love of God. That's why God is known as a God of second chances, third chances, and infinitely more chances. He always welcomes us if we humbly seek Him and obey His word. So tell your friend to do as mentioned above, and God will have mercy on him and forgive him. Just tell him not to go back to his old way of life again.

Questions to ponder:

How would you help the kid in this story?

What would you do and say?

Is there hope for kids to change bad behavior to good behavior?

God welcomes us with open arms.

JOURNAL:

_____

_____

_____

_____

_____

_____

_____

_____

_____

_____

_____

_____

_____

_____

_____

_____

_____

_____

_____

_____

_____

DECEMBER 20

Q: I have always been a good kid, respectful and loving to my family and everyone else. I had two mid-term exams on the same day that were worth 50% of my final grade. I knew I could easily study for one class and just look over the material for the other class. The class I studied for was the first class of the day, and I felt pretty good about it. The next class was my second exam, and I didn't feel very confident about it. I sit next to my friend who is extremely smart. I started on the test and felt I was doing very well, especially on the essay, but I was truly struggling on the multiple-choice portion of the test. My friend's paper was in full view (not on purpose), so I looked over and copied her answers and completed the test. I felt really bad because I usually don't cheat, but it was only one section of the test.

> **What God Says:** Luke 16:10 *Unless you are faithful in small matters, you won't be faithful in large ones. If you cheat even a little, you won't be honest with greater responsibilities.**

A: You see, unfortunately the way God looks at things, a sin is a sin. Cheating a little or cheating on the entire test is still cheating and wrong in the eyes of our Lord. Like He says in the verse above, if you are going to cheat on the little things and get away with it, what will stop you from cheating again on bigger things now that you have rationalized it in your heart. There is no way to justify sin. We all try to convince ourselves that it's no big deal. That makes our hearts hard when a similar situation arises. What you need to do is confess your sin to God and ask Him for forgiveness. And you need to tell the teacher exactly what happened and live with the consequences. Always remember that God will bless you for doing the right thing, even if it hurts us in the short run.

Questions to ponder:

If needed, would you cheat?

If yes, how would you fix that problem?

If no, how do you know?

Give examples

A little sin is still a sin.

JOURNAL:

_____

_____

_____

_____

_____

_____

_____

_____

_____

_____

_____

_____

_____

_____

_____

_____

_____

_____

_____

_____

_____

_____

_____

_____

APATHY

Q: Ever since my brother died in a car accident, I just can't seem to find any energy or emotion for anything. The accident was about three months ago, and my body is still numb over it. Since then, I haven't eaten very much, and my sleep is erratic. I quit the basketball team because I lost interest in it. I just have a hard time doing anything. Nothing seems to make sense to me. I just don't seem to have any feelings for anything. Last night, my mom and I watched our favorite tear-jerker movie, and I couldn't cry. My dad got me concert tickets to my favorite band that was playing at the amphitheater in my neighborhood, but I had no interest in going. I need to get over my apathy because it's killing me inside and making everyone around me miserable and worried about me.

> **What God Says:** 2 Timothy 1:7 *"God has not given us a spirit of fear and timidity, but of power, love, and self-discipline."*

A: You are still grieving over the loss of your brother. But there comes a time that you need to move on with your life. Apathy is a very dangerous thing because it robs you of all the love and feelings you can experience in your young life. Apathy takes away the joy that life can bring. It turns love and caring into indifference and thoughtlessness. It is the opposite of what God teaches. He has blessed us with love, power, and hope. Apathy strips us of all that and instills fear and lifelessness in our souls. You need to turn to God for strength and courage to stand up to this apathetic attitude and replace it with caring and compassion. Let God help you become the person you were before your brother's unfortunate accident. I'm sure he would want you to do the same.

Questions to ponder:
Do you ever feel apathetic?
What would make you apathetic?
How would you try to overcome it?

Keep your spirit strong, not apathetic.

JOURNAL:

DECEMBER 22

DEALING WITH BORING FRIENDS

Q: I have been best friends with this one kid in school for as long as I can remember. I used to go to his house all the time on the weekends. We would play football and baseball and have fun on his swing. We always had a good time. But now, since we've both turned 14, it is different when I go to his house. All he ever wants to do is play the same boring video game for hours and play with his dog. After about 10 minutes at his house, I am so bored that I want to go home. No more football or sports. No fishing or playing at the park. He does nothing but play that dumb video game and hang out with his mutt. I still like him as a friend because of the memories of past good times, but how can I get him to change back to the way he was before?

> **What God Says:** Ephesians 5:1–2 *Follow God's example in everything you do. Live a life filled with love for others, following the example of Christ.**

A: Nobody likes going over to a friend's house to be bored. I'm not sure what's going on with your friend, but there are a couple things you can do. First, before you go to his house, have a plan of activities to do when you get there. If he doesn't want to do any of them, then don't go over to his house. Find other friends you can have fun with. If you are a follower of God's word, there is no way you can become bored, because God instills the Holy Spirit in you who fills your heart with love and joy to serve others, and you can never get bored. You will always have plenty of ideas and things to do while serving God's people. That's what the above verse means. I would continue to try to suggest things to do with your friend, and maybe when you don't come by as often, he'll get the hint that he needs to get more active.

Questions to ponder:

Do you have a boring friend?

If yes, how did you handle him or her?

If no, how would you handle him or her?

Let the Holy Spirit instill enthusiasm in your heart.

JOURNAL: _____

_____
_____
_____
_____
_____
_____
_____
_____
_____
_____
_____
_____
_____
_____
_____
_____
_____
_____
_____
_____
_____
_____

SLOBS

Q: My mom and dad are constantly on my back to clean my room. I don't understand it because it is my room, my space, so why do I have to make it clean? I like a messy room because it has that lived-in look. I usually leave my dirty clothes on the floor, so they sometimes get mixed up with my clean clothes that are also on the floor. I also love to eat in my room while I'm listening to music. But I rarely want to clean up. So my mom finds dirty dishes and glasses along with paper plates and napkins all over the floor. When I have this clutter, I put my important stuff under my bed so it's separate from my junk. My closet is a little sloppy because I forget to put my clothes on hangers, so they, too, usually end up on the floor. Why can't my parents just close my door and let me live the way I want?

What God Says: Hebrews 10:22 *"For our guilty consciences have been sprinkled with Christ's blood to make us clean, and our bodies have been washed with pure water."*

A: They don't let you live like you want because your parents know it is not right to live like a pig. Being a slob is just another form of laziness. You are just too lazy to clean up after yourself. If God had wanted us to be slobs, why would He have created trashcans and hangars and closets? Why would He create dishwashers and soap to wash dishes? He did that so we don't have to be slobs and can live in a clean environment. God expects everything about us to be clean, as the verse above suggests. From clean bodies to clean mind to clean environments, God expects us to be clean! Again, our bodies must be clean. Our space must be clean, and our heart and soul must also be clean from all impurities. Don't be lazy. Take care of your room as God takes care of His people.

Questions to ponder:

From a scale of 1 to 10 (1 = no slob; 10 = big slob), how would you rate the sloppiness of your room?

Explain in detail.

A slob is someone justifying his or her laziness.

JOURNAL:

DEALING WITH SELFISH FRIENDS

Q: Have you ever had a friend who always had to get her way? Unfortunately, that describes one of my good friends. She's a great friend and very caring, but when she wants something or wants to go somewhere, only her way is acceptable. For example, one day a group of us were walking home from a football game, and we were all hungry. There was a fast-food hamburger place right up the street, so we decided to go there. But my friend did not want hamburgers—she wanted pizza. When we all told her no, she threw this huge fit, almost to the point of tears. We decided to go to the pizza place to keep peace and so we wouldn't be embarrassed at the other place. And she does this with everything all the time. If she doesn't get her way, she throws a fit.

What God Says: 1 Timothy 6:6 *Yet true religion with contentment is great wealth.**

A: It sounds like you have a spoiled brat as a friend. I'm just confused how someone who acts so immature could be loving and caring? She's a spoiled kid who probably always gets her way at home by throwing little tantrums. What you should have done is go to the fast-food place and let her make a fool out of herself. It might have been slightly embarrassing for the rest of you, but maybe she would have learned that she can't always get her way. Every time she acts spoiled, you and the rest of the group need to ignore her and not include her in your plans until she learns how to behave correctly. God teaches us in the verse above that being a follower of God, coupled with being content with the things that happen in your life, is worth more than money. Teach her the value of contentment and compromise, as the Lord teaches us.

Questions to ponder:

Do you have a spoiled brat as a friend?
How do you handle them?
Are you spoiled?

> Let's do things God's way, not our way.

JOURNAL: _____

_____

_____

_____

_____

_____

_____

_____

_____

_____

_____

_____

_____

_____

_____

_____

_____

_____

_____

_____

DECEMBER 25

QUESTIONS ABOUT JESUS

Q: This is Christmas Day, the day Jesus was born on earth. My family enjoys celebrating Christmas, and we always go to church to rejoice in the birth of Christ. But as I've gotten older, I have started to question things about Jesus. I have read the New Testament, but how do we know for sure that Jesus is God? From books I've read and movies I've seen, Jesus was a man just like my dad. So how do we know for sure that He is really God? And are we really sure that He died on the cross like it says in the Bible and then rose again in three days? If He died on a Friday (Good Friday) and was alive on Sunday (Easter Sunday), isn't that only two days and not three? How do we know absolutely that what is written about Jesus is correct and accurate?

What God Says: Matthew 17:5 *"A voice from the cloud said, 'This is my dearly beloved Son, who brings me great joy. Listen to him.'"*

A: We know that Jesus is God's son because God tells us that in the Bible. In the verse above at the Transfiguration, when Jesus appeared with Moses and Elijah, God spoke through the clouds and said those words. It was a direct statement from God that Jesus was His son. There were three witnesses at this event, namely Peter, James, and John. They talk about this event in other writings in the Bible. If this were not true, why would they have recorded these events in multiple places in the Bible? Too many people have tried to disprove the Bible, and no one has been successful. In fact, many atheists and agnostics have been converted to Christianity after researching the Bible and finding out how true the Bible is. So there is no need to question the events that are written in the Bible. All you need to do is believe in your heart that Jesus is Lord and that he is our savior.

Questions to ponder:
If Jesus were sitting next to you, what three questions would you ask Him? Explain your reasons for the questions.

The Bible is true and accurate.
Jesus is the Son of God.

JOURNAL:_____

_____

_____

_____

_____

_____

_____

_____

_____

_____

_____

_____

_____

_____

_____

_____

_____

_____

_____

_____

_____

_____

_____

_____

DECEMBER 26

BEING IN THE MIDDLE OF FIGHTS WITH FRIENDS

Q: I have two best friends who have totally opposite personalities. We have all been best friends for about three years, but when those two friends begin to fight, I am always in the middle of it. One friend confides in me on her side, and then the other friend confides in me on her side, and they want me to choose sides. I absolutely hate that because I love them both and I don't want to hurt either of them. Most of their fights are stupid anyway. Like the other day, one of them wanted to see a certain movie, and the other one wanted to go to a school football game, and as usual, I was in the middle. I really love my two friends a lot, but I'm getting sick and tired of being in the middle of their bickering. What can I do?

> **What God Says:** Isaiah 33:22 *"For the LORD is our judge, our lawgiver, and our king. He will care for us and save us."*

A: Fighting over silly things is a total waste of time. But putting you in the middle of these squabbles is just wrong. You are not the judge or the mediator of your friends' petty arguments. You need to sit down with both of them and tell them you have no interest in being put in the middle of their fights. It's not right for them to put you in a position to have to choose sides. Tell them that there's only one judge, one arbitrator, and one authority, and that's God. If they have a dispute, give it to God. And tell them to stop all this useless bickering. If you are all friends, just compromise. Go to the football game this weekend and see the movie the next weekend. There is always an easy solution to every petty fight when you compromise.

Question to ponder:
If you were the girl in this story, how would you handle this situation?

The world needs more loving and less fighting.

JOURNAL:

DECEMBER 27

RULES

Q: I'm getting sick and tired of all the rules in my life. I have a ton of rules at home, like being in bed by 10:00 p.m. on school nights and eating all my vegetables before dessert. There are rules in my house for everything, and if I break a rule, I get grounded for a week or can't watch TV for two weeks. Then I go to school, and there are a ton more rules I must obey. There are rules like no gum chewing on campus or wearing baggy pants or wearing a chain around my waist. There are rules in the classroom, rules at lunch, and rules after school. I'm just getting tired of people throwing all their rules in my face. I wish I could do what I want as long as I'm not hurting anyone. Why do we have so many rules?

What God Says: 2 Timothy 2:5 *For the Lord has rules for doing His work just as an athlete either follows the rules or is disqualified and wins no prize.**

A: I don't think anyone likes having rules, but they are necessary. Think for a moment how chaotic this world would be if we had no rules. If everyone were allowed to do as they pleased, this world would be full of chaos. Rules are made to establish order and so no one gets hurt or has an advantage over another. Your parents make rules to teach you right from wrong. They exist mostly for your own well-being and safety. The same is true for school. If there were no rules at school, it would be a total mess with no control. God is in favor of rules. He gives us rules to live by in the Bible (the Ten Commandments, the Golden Rule, etc.). You may not understand why certain rules are in place, but I guarantee you, it's for your own good or the safety of others.

Questions to ponder:
Name five rules at home that you hate. Why?
Name five rules at school that you hate. Why?

Rules are necessary to maintain order.

JOURNAL:

EATING THE RIGHT FOODS

Q: I am a finicky eater. I really don't like most foods, but I eat them so I don't get in trouble. The problem is that I only like eating stuff that is not good for me. I love candy, cookies, and ice cream more than anything else. I don't like any kind of vegetable or meat. Most of the time, I try to sneak most of my dinner to my dog so my mom thinks I finished my plate. Then I can get a big dessert. Another thing I do is eat a very small dinner, like a bowl of cereal, and then when everybody is out of the kitchen, I sneak in and grab some cookies or potato chips and sneak back to my room. I can live off of junk food for my entire life. So why does my mom force me to eat all this other stuff that I don't like?

What God Says: John 6:55–56 *For My flesh is the true food, and My blood is the true drink. All who eat My flesh and drink My blood remain in Me and I in them.**

A: Wouldn't it be wonderful if we could go through life eating nothing but junk food and sweets every day all the time? It may be great for a while, but you may die an early death. See, all those gross foods like vegetables and fruits are full of vitamins and minerals to help your body grow and stay healthy. All junk food and sweets are good for is a big gut and bad teeth. God teaches us that we must also have the right spiritual food and drink for our soul. We must feed it with the right amount of God's word and serving others in order to keep our soul healthy. Junk food to the body is like anger and meanness to the soul. It may be satisfying in the short term, but it will kill you later on. Feed on God's word, and keep your body and soul healthy.

Questions to ponder:

What is your favorite food?

What junk food do you eat the most?

Do you feed on God's word for food for the soul? How often? Explain.

Get your daily dose of God's word for your soul.

JOURNAL:

_____

_____

_____

_____

_____

_____

_____

_____

_____

_____

_____

_____

_____

_____

_____

_____

_____

_____

_____

_____

_____

_____

_____

DECEMBER 29

BEING SUPERSTITIOUS

Q: I am extremely superstitious, especially when something good happens. For example, if I have a good day at school or our team wins in baseball, I won't change my underwear or socks until I have a bad day. Before every baseball game, I go through the same exact routine so I don't have any bad luck. I eat the same things before each game at the same time. When I go to the training room, I put on my uniform the same way, especially if we are on a winning streak. I'm afraid if I do anything differently, my good luck will run out and we will lose the game. And it would be my fault.

> **What God Says:** 2 Thessalonians 2:11–12 *So God will send great deception on them, and they will believe all those lies. Then they will be condemned for not believing the truth and for enjoying the evil they do.**

A: I really hate to break this to you, but the only thing you are doing by not changing your underwear or socks is stinking up the place. Success has nothing to do with what socks and underwear you are wearing. The one who is going to win the baseball game is the team that plays the best. Don't believe in these superstitious lies. Again, it doesn't matter what you eat or what time you eat before a game, because it doesn't mean anything. God hates it when people believe in superstitious lies. They are like the great deception described in the verse above. The way to win your baseball games is to practice hard and give 100% effort, and whatever happens, happens. Instead of believing in superstitious lies, put your trust in God to have a good day or a good game. Start your routine with a prayer to Him before each game. God will condemn those who put their faith in false ideas and not in Him.

Questions to ponder:

Are you superstitious?

Why or why not?

Do you have friends who are superstitious?

Does it bother you?

Being superstitious is like following a false god.

JOURNAL:

_____

_____

_____

_____

_____

_____

_____

_____

_____

_____

_____

_____

_____

_____

_____

_____

_____

_____

_____

_____

_____

_____

DECEMBER 30

LIFE AS AN ORPHAN

Q: I was raised like an orphan. My dad left town as soon as he found out my mom was pregnant. My mom had no money and very little family, so she thought it was best to have the baby (me) and then immediately give me up for adoption. So I was put in the foster care system for about three years until a family decided to adopt me. The family is nice with a mom and a dad and two other kids, but I get a strange feeling that I just don't belong. I don't feel like their child, even though they treat me well. I feel like an outsider. Many times, I get the feeling that I am unloved because my real mom didn't want me. I don't understand how a mom could ever give up her child. Why would she hate me so much?

> **What God Says:** 1 John 3:1 *How great is the love the father has lavished on us that we should be called children of God. And that is what we are.**

A: To God, no child is an orphan, and no child is hated. All of God's children are loved unconditionally. I can understand your confusion about what your real mom did. But 99.9% of moms love their kids, and she must have done this for your best interest, to give you the best possible life that she couldn't give you. It must have been as difficult for her to do that as it is for you to accept it. She probably put your well-being ahead of her personal feelings, and that is extremely unselfish. You should never feel unloved or unwanted. You have adoptive parents who want you and love you. You have a real mom who loves you enough to do what she thought was best for you. And you have a father in heaven who loves you tremendously and is watching over you. Talk to your adoptive parents about your feelings, but more than that, talk to God and ask Him to help you understand the confusion you're feeling. Pray for comfort and wisdom in your situation.

Questions to ponder:
What would change in your life if you found out you were adopted?
How would your feelings change?
Would you be bitter?
Explain.

There are no orphans in God's eyes.

JOURNAL:

_____

_____

_____

_____

_____

_____

_____

_____

_____

_____

_____

_____

_____

_____

_____

_____

_____

_____

_____

_____

_____

_____

DECEMBER 31

NIGHTMARES

Q: I suffer from terrible nightmares. It all started when I witnessed this guy attempt to rape and physically abuse a woman. I was walking home from my friend's house and heard screaming behind a building. I went to check it out and saw a man get physical with a young woman. I got scared because I didn't want to be seen. Suddenly, I heard the siren of an ambulance, which must have scared the man a bit because he ran off. By that time, I was running as fast as I could back to my house. But since then, for the last month, I've been having nightmares of men attacking me just like that girl was attacked. When it gets dark, I get scared. I'm deathly afraid to close my eyes and go to sleep. I haven't told anyone what I saw because I'm afraid the man might try to hurt me.

What God Says: Psalm 56:3 *"But when I am afraid, I will put my trust in you."*

A: I figure you've been holding this inside of you since you witnessed this crime. Those nightmares you are having are flashbacks from that night. To get rid of the flashbacks, you need to do two things: first, you need to put all your trust in God to get rid of the nightmares and, more importantly, to get rid of the fear. And second, you need to talk to as many qualified people as you can, starting with your parents. To conquer fear, you need to get this fear out in the open where it can be dealt with. But it all starts with God, because he will give you the courage to face those fears head on and help you get rid of them. Nightmares are scary for both old and young people alike, and there's nothing worse than the fear of closing your eyes to go to sleep. Trust God and do this now so you can rest.

Questions to ponder:
Do you occasionally suffer from nightmares?
If yes, how do you try to get rid of them?
If no, how would you try to get rid of them?

God can help you get a good night's sleep.

JOURNAL:

The life lessons I have learned this month are:

_____

_____

_____

_____

_____

_____

_____

_____

_____

_____

_____

_____

_____

_____

_____

_____

_____

_____

_____

_____

_____

_____

_____

_____

_____

APPENDIX 1: BOOK CATEGORIES
LISTED ALPHABETICALLY

Month	Day	Title
November	19	Advising good kids with bad intentions
November	24	Advising kids who want to pierce their bodies
December	21	Apathy
October	26	Arguing
December	26	Being in the middle of fights with friends
December	29	Being superstitious
December	1	Burdens
November	2	Changing behavior
December	20	Cheating
October	19	Comforting a sad friend
November	26	Comforting kids who are deeply depressed
November	3	Comforting kids with grief
October	2	Communication with parents
December	16	Controlling lustful thoughts
October	27	Dealing with a bitter friend
November	18	Dealing with arrogant kids
December	22	Dealing with boring friends
October	5	Dealing with emotional friends
October	8	Dealing with friends full of excuses
December	24	Dealing with selfish friends
October	25	Dealing with friends who won't admit they are wrong
December	14	Dealing with friends who nag

October	30	Dealing with friends who talk loudly
October	11	Dealing with kids who can't love
October	3	Dealing with overly competitive kids
November	16	Dealing with person contemplating suicide
October	18	Dealing with stubborn friends
December	17	Dealing with unforgiving friends
October	4	Disability
October	24	Disappointment
November	28	Doubts about God
October	10	Doubts about self
December	2	Drinking and drugs
December	28	Eating the right foods
November	21	Evil thoughts from others
October	7	Family issues
December	13	Forgetfulness
November	7	Friends with parent problems
December	7	Gluttony
November	27	Good judgment
October	9	Grudges
November	22	Heaven
October	23	Helping a friend through trials
November	17	Helping a friend who can't trust
November	11	Helping a friend who wants to run away
November	1	Helping friends deal with anger
December	6	Helping friends who feel bad about themselves
December	18	Helping friends who get yelled at a lot
November	20	Helping friends who need to be cool
December	15	Helping friends with a guilty conscience
December	3	Helping kids at a new school
October	6	Helping kids make good decisions
December	19	Helping kids get back on track with their Christianity
October	28	Helping kids who are greedy
November	8	Helping kids who are obsessed
December	9	Helping kids who feel like failures
November	25	Helping kids who want what other people have

December	11	How to deal with a chatterbox
December	12	How to deal with friends becoming enemies
December	5	Insincere kids
December	8	Kids who despise for no reason
November	29	Kids with big egos
November	4	Kids with gay feelings
December	10	Laziness
December	30	Life as an orphan
October	29	Like the same boy or girl
December	4	Loneliness
October	12	Lying to cover wrongdoing
November	30	Making smart choices
November	5	Motivating those kids who are unmotivated
December	31	Nightmares
November	6	No sense of humor
October	1	Oppression at school
October	13	Overweight and glasses
November	23	Prayer
November	10	Pride
October	20	Problems with the law
October	15	Procrastination
December	25	Questions about Jesus
October	31	Quitting
November	9	Rebellious kids
October	14	Retaliation
November	12	Risk
December	27	Rules
November	15	Sexual thoughts
November	13	Showing friends how to say no to others
October	17	Sibling problems
December	23	Slobs
October	16	Tattling brothers and sisters
November	14	Terminal illness
October	21	Threats
October	22	Wasting time, doing nothing

APPENDIX 2: THOUGHTS FOR THE DAY

Month	Day	Thought for the Day
October	1	Ask God to strengthen your faith.
October	2	Don't shun communication with your parents.
October	3	Don't be cocky or judgmental when you win.
October	4	Positively accept the things you cannot change.
October	5	You need to be there when your friend is hurting.
October	6	Taking good advice usually leads to wise decisions.
October	7	God wants a dad to be the leader in his family.
October	8	There are no excuses with God.
October	9	Grudges can ruin a person's soul.
October	10	God gives us the confidence to handle anything.
October	11	To love God, you must love all His people.
October	12	Using people to cover your sin is a hideous act.
October	13	Rely on God's power against mean kids.
October	14	God loves peace, not war.
October	15	Time has a way of flying by—don't procrastinate.
October	16	Tattling at a young age is normally fool's talk.
October	17	Be patient and humble with your siblings.
October	18	Don't live with a stubborn heart.
October	19	With God, s-a-d is just two letters from being g-l-a-d.
October	20	Pray to God to deliver you from evil.
October	21	God's strength is more powerful than human threats.
October	22	Opportunity missed is an opportunity lost.
October	23	God rejoices when you turn to Him in your time of trials.

October	24	Losing is always disappointing, but God can lift our spirits.
October	25	Admitting failure is not a sign of weakness.
October	26	There is a compromise for every argument.
October	27	Bitterness makes you feel hatred and anger inside.
October	28	Don't be greedy with your material things.
October	29	Don't choose a girlfriend or boyfriend over a true friend.
October	30	Use a loud voice to praise God.
October	31	Don't quit praising God. He will never quit on you.
November	1	Handle conflicts with kindness and gentleness.
November	2	To change your behavior, you need to change your heart.
November	3	God is the ultimate source of comfort.
November	4	Seek God when you are confused about your sexuality.
November	5	Find your skill and do it.
November	6	Don't rob your soul of laughter.
November	7	Your parents deserve your honor and respect.
November	8	Be obsessed with being a Christ-pleaser.
November	9	Don't rebel against God's commands, for the penalty is death.
November	10	Turn your pride into humility.
November	11	If you need to run, run toward God.
November	12	Living your life for God is no risk.
November	13	Say no to wrong; say yes to God.
November	14	Don't blame God for your illnesses.
November	15	You can control your mind with God's help.
November	16	Don't ever destroy what God has created.
November	17	Trust God and put your confidence in Him.
November	18	You can't walk with God if you are self-absorbed.
November	19	Don't pray for bad will against others.
November	20	Be cool with God and not the devil.
November	21	Only God has the power to change evil to good.
November	22	Invite Jesus into your heart for the pathway to heaven.
November	23	Pray with a humble and contrite heart.
November	24	Your body belongs to God; do what He says is good.
November	25	Ask humbly for your needs, and you shall receive.
November	26	Depression to joy may be just a prayer away.
November	27	Strong will and character lead to good judgment.

November	28	God's comfort is greater than our suffering.
November	29	E.G.O: Earning God's Outrage.
November	30	All smart choices begin and end with God.
December	1	God is the perfect medicine for the burdened soul.
December	2	Fill your body with the Holy Spirit.
December	3	God is proud when we deny ourselves to help others.
December	4	With God, you are never alone.
December	5	Be true and sincere with everyone.
December	6	You are a priceless treasure in the eyes of God.
December	7	Gluttony is the opposite of self-control.
December	8	Don't despise anyone; love one another.
December	9	To God, we only fail if we don't trust Him.
December	10	Lazy kids usually turn into lazy adults.
December	11	A tongue can pierce hearts like a sword.
December	12	You may hate his deeds, but you must love your neighbor.
December	13	Change this bad habit of forgetfulness.
December	14	Be persistent and humble in prayer. Do not nag.
December	15	A sincere apology is the medicine for a guilty conscience.
December	16	Lustful thoughts lead to sexual action.
December	17	Always be humble when asking for forgiveness.
December	18	People listen much better when the yelling stops.
December	19	God welcomes us with open arms.
December	20	A little sin is still a sin.
December	21	Keep your spirit strong, not apathetic.
December	22	Let the Holy Spirit instill enthusiasm in your heart.
December	23	A slob is someone justifying his or her laziness.
December	24	Let's do things God's way, not our way.
December	25	The Bible is true and accurate. Jesus is the Son of God..
December	26	The world needs more loving and less fighting.
December	27	Rules are necessary to maintain order.
December	28	Get your daily dose of God's word for your soul.
December	29	Being superstitious is like following a false god.
December	30	There are no orphans in God's eyes.
December	31	God can help you get a good night's sleep.

www.ingramcontent.com/pod-product-compliance
Lightning Source LLC
Chambersburg PA
CBHW071428090426
42737CB00011B/1603